TESTIMONIALS

Most first-time job searches are haphazard and opportunistic at best, to the graduate's significant detriment. In this book, William makes a case for purposeful planning and critical evaluation when pursuing that initial position after college. He brings a perspective worth understanding before staring down your first interviewer.

Deane Barker
Author, Speaker, and Chief Strategy Officer at Blend Interactive

The best developers I know are those who almost always have some kind of side project. There's only so much that can be taught in school, therefore a strong history of pet projects is one of the best ways I gauge the capabilities and fit of potential new hires. I love it when I can learn something new from someone looking to join our team. I honestly don't think it's possible for me to hire a software engineer who doesn't have a side project they can share during an interview—it's just that important.

Travis Kiefer
President of Kiefer Enterprise

As a former K-12 educator and University Dean, I understand the importance of training and graduating Computer Science majors. The employment opportunities are expanding rapidly and it is incumbent on our education system to prepare students for opportunities in this dynamic field. William's book provides the motivation and insight necessary for Computer Science candidates to prepare for a career in this exciting profession.

Rick Melmer
Leadership South Dakota

Code or be coded! Having the ability to write code will be your key to unlock incredible value for yourself and others in the 21st century. In this book, William gives you the step-by-guide to start down the path of code pro.

John T. Meyer
Co-Founder at Lemonly

Introducing more women in computer science and technology can help spur creativity and innovation. *Wired For Coding* does an excellent job of providing information so women can leverage William's experience to jump start their future in development and technology. The book goes beyond coding to career advice and professional etiquette.

Ashley Podhradsky, D.Sc
Associate Professor of Digital Forensics and Information Assurance
Coordinator of Masters of Science in IA and Computer Security
GenCyber Girls Camp Director | www.gencybergirls.camp
Dakota State University

The lessons found in *Wired For Coding* are essential for new graduates. William shares perspectives from the employer which aren't found in typical computer science curriculum. Even established technology pros will benefit from reading this book.

Ryan Sougstad, Ph.D.
Associate Professor
Business Administration and Computer Information Systems
Augustana University
Sioux Falls, SD

Wired For Coding sets up a perfect framework for successfully transitioning from college to career. From setting goals to building a personal brand, William's book outlines exactly how to portray what employers are looking for in high-potential hires. As someone who has interviewed and hired developers, I can promise that following even some of William's advice will give job seekers a distinct advantage. Read it by your second year in college and take control of your career.

Sara Steever
President of Paulsen Marketing

A college education is only the beginning of what you'll need to be a developer in the real world, and William is passionate about helping you get the skills to succeed in the career of your dreams.

Sarah Rhea Werner
Host of the *Write Now Podcast* and Senior Content Strategist at Click Rain

WIRED FOR CODING

WILLIAM BUSHEE

Coming soon in the *Wired For* series

Wired For Design
Wired For Marketing

For your free *Wired For Coding* worksheet guide,
visit http://wiredforcoding.com/worksheet

WIRED FOR CODING

HOW TO STAND OUT FROM THE CROWD AND LAND YOUR FIRST JOB AS A DEVELOPER

WILLIAM BUSHEE

THRONE
PUBLISHING GROUP

Throne Publishing Group
2329 N Career Ave #215
Sioux Falls, SD 57107
ThronePG.com

TABLE OF CONTENTS

INTRODUCTION

This book was written specifically for students in college who want to begin a career as a software engineer, developer, coder, code ninja, or whatever you want to call yourself. I simply use the title "developer." Those pursuing careers in other fields will also find the information valuable but will need to come up with their own portfolio variations based on the industry. You can also read other books in the *Wired* series for one that matches your career field.

So you want to be a developer? That's fantastic, because it's a wonderful career choice with myriad directions and potential. There are so many options for careers: writing back-end code to operate process, writing front-end code making beautiful interfaces, developing mobile applications, writing education platforms, developing your own software, or even writing video games. But even if you end up never writing a single line of production-level code, you can apply your valuable development skills to other professions—such as sales, marketing, design, support, and any sector of commerce or industry. My experience shows that those who understand how software works have significantly greater success at marketing, selling, and servicing software. For example, marketing project managers who can talk deeper with their clients about how the development team will implement their solutions. Sales managers who can accurately determine solutions with their customers without needing to check with their support team.

There is more to being a developer than writing code. The more you understand about marketing, sales, and business, the more opportunities will open in your career as well. I strongly believe that the more everyone understands about how software works, the better they are at their specific jobs. No one is immune to computers, technology, or the Internet in today's world. Every profession and career leverages technology, and technology's pervasiveness and usefulness will only keep growing. You have chosen wisely to pursue a computer science career, regardless of how you actually practice your skills. The more you know about technology, the more value you bring your employer, which directly translates into more opportunities and more money for you.

Before I dive deep into the process I developed for you to leverage your degree, let's talk about why you want to become a developer. I hope the answer isn't because someone told you it was a good career, or because you knew someone else who chose that path, or your guidance counselor suggested it. Just like everything in life, if you do not have passion for what you are doing, you will probably be unhappy. This makes it important that you have a passion for your field. And there are plenty of different areas you might have a passion for in which you can leverage your new skills.

As someone who teaches developers and runs a business that hires all levels of developers, I know a few things about what employers are looking for in new employees. Plus, I have over twenty years of experience with developers. And I always say, don't just learn to code—learn to become a developer.

What I mean by this is that knowing the fundamentals of writing code is completely different from being a developer. There is so much more to being a developer than simply knowing the syntax and language and having the knowledge of a programming language—knowing the "how" and "why" is far more important than knowing the "what." Any traditional computer science program will teach you the "what," because that is the easy part. But understanding the "how" and "why" comes in only two ways—either you naturally understand technology (rare) or you build the knowledge through experience (more common). Both are perfectly acceptable ways to become a true developer, and each method comes with its own rewards, timelines, and career options.

Graduating with a computer science degree does not automatically translate into you being a developer. That will come, but it will not be automatic, despite what your college adviser might have told you when you selected your degree. To become an expert at something, it is estimated that you need to commit 10,000 hours to that skill—or five years of forty-hour weeks. A solid understanding of your field, a focused approach to beginning your career, and presenting yourself well as you network and interview for your top-choice jobs will help you reach that goal of becoming a great developer.

It is very expensive for a business to hire someone, especially someone with no experience. College graduates often start off not knowing what businesses need, without a strong skill set, and having little practical experience. But this book can give you strong strategies for addressing all of those issues and positioning yourself to start your career off strong and on track to a fulfilling, successful career in software engineering.

Hopefully, this book will find you early in your college journey, ideally during your sophomore or junior year. Like all journeys, one that is planned out well and organized will be more successful than a journey spontaneously taken with no direction and no guidance. This book is about building that plan, setting goals, and executing those goals in a timely manner.

I recommend starting this journey as early as possible for two reasons:

1. Starting early proves you are serious and passionate about your career.
2. Starting early gives you time to develop a solid plan, build a robust portfolio, and gain real-world experience.

This book is not about interviewing, although I will cover interviewing basics. It's not about how to find a job, it's not about picking a career, and it's not about writing a résumé. There are plenty of other books dedicated to each of those topics, and you should also read those. This book is about what prospective employers in the coding field are looking for in recent graduates or entry-level developers, and how you need to prepare to meet the expectations necessary to land the career you want.

After all, you have already committed at least four years in college to getting that computer science (or similar) degree. You don't want to end up getting a job you absolutely hate just because you didn't put in the time and effort to land the job you really wanted. Don't look back twenty years from now and wonder why you didn't put in the necessary effort.

There's a huge demand for new computer science graduates, and you need to set yourself apart from the crowd so you can control the job offers, and therefore your career path. Don't leave it to chance, faith, or necessity when finding a career.

Even though there is a huge demand for technology jobs, every job is not the same. If you are passionate about landing a job writing video games, you need to set yourself apart from the pack as someone who already possesses the skills and experience necessary to hit the ground running. Businesses don't want to hire an entry-level employee and spend six to eight months (or even several years) training them only to find out it's not working and have to fire them. Those are expenses no employer wants to incur. I will show you how to take advantage of this concern by building a custom portfolio geared specifically to the type of career you want after graduation. It's not hard, but does take work and planning.

As vice president of development at BrightPlanet, a data harvesting company in Sioux Falls, South Dakota, I manage our team of senior developers and oversee all the technology and innovation that goes into BrightPlanet's data harvesting engine. I've spent years working with software engineers of all experience levels, and I've also spent years interviewing too many college students to count. My experience in those two areas has given me access to knowledge and numerous strategies that will help you get started in the industry.

I've been with BrightPlanet since it was founded in 2001, where I served as the lead engineer and oversaw the inception of our harvest platform. The Internet has changed substantially since those days, not only in size but also sophistication. I've worked with many open-source and private technology companies doing innovative things with data.

At BrightPlanet, I'm the go-to guy for software engineering, managing teams, and understanding the roles technologies play in business success. I am an expert in open-source intelligence, deep web harvesting, web crawling, and unstructured data collection and management.

I volunteer my years of experience as a director on three boards: Health Connect of South Dakota, Computers for the Community, and a Dakota State University advisory board. As an avid technologist, I help keep these organizations up to speed with the ever-changing technology landscape. Networking and volunteering are key parts of a successful career, as you'll see discussed in a later chapter.

In 2010, I founded South Dakota Geeks, the largest South Dakota technology group on LinkedIn, to provide a community dedicated to those less-social engineers. The group quickly grew to more than five hundred members who regularly attend socials geared toward geeks.

Participating in these kinds of groups is essential for career support, developing opportunities, and keeping yourself connected to the field.

BlueMonkey Development provides my consulting, advisory services, mentorship, and subject matter expertise platform where I blog (albeit infrequently), interact with early-stage companies, and provide guidance to those who ask. The benefits of platforms like this are significant, and I'll discuss those in depth in the networking and experience chapters.

In 2014, I cofounded Code Bootcamp of South Dakota. Code Bootcamp teaches web development to students over an intense, twelve-week program that includes mentorship, networking, life skills, and everything they will need to start a career as entry-level developers. Code Bootcamp quickly spawned a suborganization called Gaming Bootcamp, geared toward educating kids from fourth to ninth grade. The boot camp was an instant success; I continue to run the events regularly today. Investing in and even founding projects like these can be fulfilling and rewarding, in addition to expanding your experience, challenging you in new ways, and building your network and opportunities.

I'm an avid technology enthusiast and a firm believer that almost any problem can be solved with a little creative thinking, with the proper dataset, or by building the correct enrichment of web data. I enjoy working with young entrepreneurs, early-stage startups, and those struggling with the latest technology.

Because starting off a career in a challenging and competitive career like software engineering can be so difficult, it's important that you start preparing now. *Wired For Coding* will help you get where you want to go.

1

FALLING INTO THE "GOOD ENOUGH" TRAP

Over the years, I have interviewed too many college students to count. I enjoy setting up a day of interviews at a local college campus and interviewing students all day, even though it is brutally exhausting. A typical interview day features eight to ten candidates in thirty-minute increments, with a few breaks for the interviewers—and always one or two no-shows, which always surprises me.

One thing that always stands out when interviewing soon-to-be or recently graduated students is that they are greatly unprepared for the workforce. This book was written to close that gap between the traditional methods of job preparation and the current reality of the job market. What employers in the software engineering field want to see in candidates is rarely what those interviewing bring to the table.

A degree alone is not sufficient to land the career you want. You probably will not find it difficult to land just any job, but is just any job what you had in mind?

My long career managing and working with developers has allowed me to work with engineers ranging from those who have no experience to those with decades of experience, and everything in between. While there is a lot to be said for experience, nothing beats bringing in a fresh graduate and training them into exactly the kind of developer your organization desires. They know exactly what you want them to know, develop to your exact policies, bring a fresh new member to the team, and can truly become part of your core team.

Being a recent graduate can be a wonderful thing, and if you know how to leverage that while still bringing what employers want to see to the interview, you can present yourself as the right person for the job you want.

Building a culture capable of morphing fresh graduates into efficient developers has been a process I have refined over the past twenty years. I am a self-proclaimed "natural-born" developer with virtually no professional training in the field. My experience was built in the trenches with great mentors and a lot of hard work, perseverance, and debugging, which has provided me with a unique perspective. This book can show you how to put in the time and effort to excel as a software developer, system administrator, program manager, and business owner.

I wrote this book so that everyone could leverage my experience in this industry to get an immediate leg up in the job market, and to land and follow a great career with ambition and direction. But before I begin our job preparation, let's take a quick look to see how your first interview will go, since you might have never been professionally interviewed before. This should help set the stage for what you are facing upon graduation.

Step 1: You will be graduating soon and need a job. You might scour the Internet for available jobs—and many of them state so many years of experience are preferred. You'll probably also ask people you know about places that may be hiring. It's also a great strategy to head over to the career center and write your name on every job interview sign-up sheet hanging on the bulletin board—but your name will be right next to fifteen other students' names, people who have the exact same experience as you. You may know absolutely nothing about the company you will eventually be interviewing with, but you're not worried since you are about to graduate with a degree in a specific discipline and you're ready to work hard and set yourself apart.

Step 2: You give your well-written résumé, printed on the finest parchment available, to the career counselor. Your résumé is exactly one page long and includes that serving job you've been working at for the last six months. It also contains a bullet list of your skills and attributes like "good listener," "motivated," and "outgoing," so you've covered all your bases.

Step 3: A few weeks later you show up at the designated time and wait your turn for the first, and probably last, interview you'll ever do. After all, you are the perfect candidate, so there's no reason not to hire you, right? You dress professionally and prepare a few talking points about your enthusiasm and work ethic to show you are serious.

Step 4: The interview is with a company you know nothing about and is conducted by two people from human resources who don't know the difference between Java and iced tea. They ask a series of standard questions—ones you have prepared for. You nail the interview. After all, you are about to graduate with the exact degree they're looking for, you're eager, and you'll go the extra mile. What more would they want?

Step 5: Except it turns out they must have wanted something more, because you never hear from them again and it appears you'll be waiting tables for the immediate future. You are completely puzzled and clueless as to why you didn't get the job. And that's fair, because you probably would make a great employee. Something just isn't coming through.

So, what was it? What happened? It's the trap of "good enough." The problem is found in Step 1. "*… right next to fifteen other students' names, people who have the exact same experience as you.*" Those odds aren't actually bad; just do fifteen interviews and the chances of landing a job increase significantly. But what if you don't want just any job? What if you want to pick the company and pick the job where you will spend the majority of every day?

Surprisingly, the process of writing your own future is not that complicated. In fact, it is very easy to set yourself apart from those other applicants, but few students know how to stand out in the ways that employers are looking for. What you need to know is what every business, or at least every successful business, is looking for in fresh college candidates to give you that edge to reach your success.

Now let's take a quick look at that same interview from the interviewer's perspective. To capture their attention, you need to know what they see during these interviews.

Depending on the size of the company, there will either be someone from human resources or someone from the department actually hiring. I'll cover proper technique during a later chapter, but surprisingly, technique has little to do with your chances of landing a job.

Step 1: A typical interview day at a college campus consists of eight to twelve students interviewing per company. Each interview lasts no longer than thirty minutes, and those conducting the interview will have only one or two breaks all day. This is brutal, so the first candidate of the day will get far more attention than the last candidate, guaranteed.

Step 2: Usually the interviewers will read your résumé just moments before you walk through the door. Every grammar mistake and spelling error will be spotted immediately. Your lack of experience is a glaring red flag, and your résumé will not stand out from any other candidate's. Think of an assembly line pumping out perfectly average gizmos—as far as they know, you're just an average gizmo.

Step 3: You walk in and introduce yourself. The interviewers confirm they have the correct résumé, because surprisingly often they will not. The first question will be about you, probably the "tell us about yourself" question. You immediately start talking about how you're a "results-oriented, hard worker" and you may stumble your way down a few random tangents. Pretty soon you're accidentally talking about your favorite vacation spots as a child. Oops. They're already bored with you—strike one.

Step 4: The interview continues with a set of technical questions and maybe a few personal questions thrown in. The only time you see the interviewer jot notes is when you screw something up. They ask what version of Java you use and you don't recall, but let's be honest, no developer would pay attention to that detail—I couldn't tell you the version I have installed on my laptop today. It doesn't matter; they are only looking for a reason to remove your name from the list so they have one fewer candidate to consider. They actually don't care about your answers either, just that you have an answer—and you did not. Strike two.

Step 5: You conclude the interview, thank them for their time, and leave the room. The two interviewers compare notes and highlight all of the reasons to eliminate you, rank you against the other candidates they have seen so far today, and then call in the next guy who is waiting patiently in the hallway, probably wearing a nicer suit.

Step 6: Tomorrow they will recommend the one or two candidates that stood out from the pack for a follow-up interview, if they even recommend anyone. After all, every candidate had the exact same education and experience. They are done. It is now someone else's problem.

So how did you do? Did you pass that first critical hurtle? Did you stand out from the pack? If not, you just ended up in the recycle bin instead of the "call-back" bin.

The problem with what happened in this situation is that candidates interviewing for positions like these often fall into the trap of *good enough*. The résumé is good enough, their experience should be good enough, their talking points are good enough. But good enough is no longer good enough. When looking for competitive positions in competitive fields, you can't afford to only be good enough.

This book will help you fix the job search problem by building experience, a strong portfolio, and the ability to write your own ticket to whichever career you desire.

Now, let's get started.

2

GOAL-SETTING AND CAREER PLANNING

Knowing how to set and accomplish goals is a key factor behind career success. For some reason, this skill is not taught in schools, so unless you were lucky to have a great mentor early in your career, you might not have focused on effective ways to set goals.

There are hundreds of books written on the topic. My favorite is *Think and Grow Rich* by Napoleon Hill. It is a short read and I highly recommend reading it. Napoleon Hill researched and interviewed more than forty millionaires for the book, which was published in 1937, and one of the common traits was setting long-term goals.

I. DEFINING AND EXECUTING YOUR GOALS

Goals need to be written down. If you don't write down your goals, they are just thoughts or dreams. Pick a specific place that you will use to write down your goals—it might be a notebook or a file on your phone or computer. It should be something that is easily accessible on a daily basis.

Goals can be immediate or long-term. The best immediate goals build toward a long-term goal. To begin setting and accomplishing these goals, start by writing down your top immediate goals—one or two or three or five or ten. The criteria for a strong goal is that it should be:

Specific, Measurable, Achievable, Relevant, and Time-bound—SMART.

Make sure your goals meet all five of those criteria. A good example of a strong goal would be:

- Send out my résumé to ten businesses over the next two weeks.
- Publish four blog posts on my portfolio website each month.
- Attend one networking event each week for six months.
- Spend less than one hour each day on social media.

Do not set unrealistic goals, because if you do, you are only setting yourself up for failure. However, be realistic about pushing yourself at the same time, and aim big. My biggest regret was not setting big enough goals when I was younger.

Measurability is also especially important. A goal cannot be "to be rich," because that is not measurable. Instead, set a goal like "make $100,000 per year within five years of graduation." That number is measurable, and that means you can review your long-term goals quarterly and annually to make sure you are on track.

Any goal not written down is not a goal. You must write down your goals and frequently review them to ensure you are making the right decisions to accomplish them. There is no magic format, style, or technique. Many people use a physical notepad or Evernote or a phone app, but it must be something that is convenient to review regularly—daily is optimal. Right before bed is a great time for personal reflection, but some like to do it early in the morning.

Once you have defined your goals, you need to review your goals every day at least once. While reviewing your goals, ask yourself what you are going to do today to move one step closer to that goal, and then take that step. For example, if you are going to write a blog post, do you have the topic selected, is there an outline defined, and can you start the draft today? Make small, 1% adjustments every day toward your goals; before you know it, they will be accomplished.

As you accomplish your goals, take pride in scratching them off the list and replacing them with new goals that build toward your bigger and more ambitious goals.

Never stop the process of setting and accomplishing goals throughout your life. If you find yourself on a life tangent, get back on track immediately. I like to reread *Think and Grow Rich* when this happens, which is usually once per year.

If you are thinking this sounds like a lot of complicated work, you are right. It's your career we are talking about. Isn't your future financial success and personal self-worth important enough to put in a little extra work? You only have so much time in life and you are trading this precious time each day for a wage; make sure you aren't selling yourself short.

Knowing which goals to set can be tough if you don't yet know where you want to go, or if you are torn between options. Goal-setting won't help you much if the goals you're setting don't take you where you want to go. It's important to know where you want to go and what you're aiming for with these goals.

So let's take some time to envision your ideal career. Finding that perfect career will require a plan, a well-thought-out plan. The first step of any well-thought-out plan is to define your goals. You don't want to rush your decision. This is a long-term career you are targeting, and it requires hours of preparing and hundreds of hours of work. Anything worth doing is worth doing right.

There are millions of jobs and career paths available. Few people know where their path lies the day they graduate college. Do not stress out about the exact job you want to do for the rest of your life; instead, focus on the culture and type of company you want to go to work for each day. Great companies are more interested in finding great employees first and finding the ideal position for them later, or building the right position for them once they come aboard. Those companies offer the best career paths.

II. TYPES OF DEVELOPMENT JOBS

Having a computer science (or similar) degree does provide you with a lot of possible job opportunities in pretty much every industry imaginable. You do not need to be one of those nerdy people who sits in the office and hacks away on the keyboard all day long with Mountain Dew, although there is nothing wrong with that type of job either.

Today you can choose from any number of industries to leverage your technical degree. In addition to working in virtually any industry, there are a number of different business types to choose from. Most technical positions fit into these types of businesses:

Traditional Development Job: This work would have you developing the business's internal software and the clients are typically other employees at the same business. This would include businesses like telecommunication or banks. Usually they have a large team of developers with a very rigid development process and hierarchy. The pay is usually good, the work is typically narrow, and the processes are going to be very strict.

Agency Work: This work would have you developing on a client's project where your time is billed to the client by the hour. You will be expected to work quickly, take shortcuts where applicable, track every hour, and work on a huge variety of projects. The pay will be competitive, the work will be broad, you will become an expert in many different areas, and the processes are usually going to be pretty loose. The business is only making money if you are billing hours.

Freelance: This work will have you performing a lot of different roles. You will be working for yourself, so you'll be doing sales, marketing, accounting, project management, and the actual client work as well. The pay is usually good, the work has a ton of variety, you only make money when you work, and if you get stuck, you won't have anyone to easily turn to.

Software/Services Company: This work will have you working on a product or service that the company sells to others, like a content management system. You will likely be working with a small team of developers directly in the production code that is being used by clients. Typically, there will be a lot of policies and procedures to follow, but if it is a young company, those might still be pretty loose. The pay is usually good, the work may be more bug fixes or small enhancements, you will have a team of other developers, and the pace may be pretty fast.

Startup/Cofounder: This work will be super fast-paced, high energy, high risk, and usually a lot of fun. The atmosphere is not for everyone, so expect to get burned out and work under tight deadlines and possibly with short budgets. Most startups fail; it's just a fact. The pay is usually poor, the work is hard, the experience is unmatched, the pace is exhausting, and the possible rewards are high.

There are other types of businesses you may work for too, but those are the common ones you'll see today. More and more developers are pursuing freelance careers because more businesses are hiring independent contractors instead of full-time developers. This is a great trend, although it does require a number of skills that are not currently taught in colleges.

Every developer is not cut out for every type of business. If one of them stands out as your passion, go for it and focus on those types of businesses. For example, I could never work for an agency because I can't cut corners and rush projects. I need every line of code to be perfect.

III. FINDING A COMPANY CULTURE THAT FITS YOU

Company culture is key, but the worst part about culture is that you can see very little about it from a job posting or interview. To evaluate a company's culture, you must know the people, know the company, and know what they stand for in their community. So do a lot of research on the companies you think you may want to work for. Culture can only be evaluated by investigating prospective companies and networking with their current and past employees. This can be done through networking events, tracking down connections through LinkedIn, or if you are brave, just showing up and asking.

If you have heard great things about a specific company and want to learn more about their culture before applying, here's a secret way to find out more—show up at their office and ask if you can hang out there for the day. You might think that is a crazy idea and if it were that simple, everyone would know about this strategy. Doing so will definitely set you apart, and there is no guarantee that they will let you in, but you might be surprised. If you showed up one day at my office, I'd welcome you with open arms, take you around, and might even give you a project.

I have talked with other business owners during the research for this book, and they all agreed that if a college student made the request to hang out for the day, they would not object. Once there, you can witness the culture firsthand, get to know who works there, and introduce yourself to the boss. And trust me, they won't forget you either. Make sure you send a handwritten thank-you note after the day you spent there, thanking them for their time.

Finding a great company culture should be a huge part of your goal for your future career path, but in addition to a positive culture, your first job should provide you with a rich career path. You need a job that allows you to grow, learn, excel, and move upward.

The great thing about making company culture and upward mobility a part of your career goal is that no matter what field you find these elements in, you'll build your skills and develop as a person. It's then fine if you decide to switch jobs, companies, or even industries throughout your career. In fact, it is healthy to do so. Just make sure every change is vertical and justified based on your career path goals; you don't want to continually make horizontal moves throughout your career.

Also, keep in mind that finding the perfect culture for you is very personal. I know businesses that have great cultures and their employees love working there, but sometimes they hire new staff members that are just not a good fit for that culture and those people end up leaving, which is fine. Some people like their culture to include a lot of socialization while others would go insane if they had to play kickball on Fridays. You need to find a culture that works for you.

When thinking about what kind of company culture you want to work for, pay attention to your positive work habits. How do you work best? Are you most motivated when part of a creative team, or do you work best on tight deadlines? Do relaxed environments give you space to think and perform well, or do fast-paced, exciting environments prompt you to do your best? What sort of management styles do you respond to best?

Taking note of your own social patterns, work habits, productivity patterns, and personal philosophies can help you determine the company culture that fits you best.

Another great strategy for determining what kind of company culture and even career path would be best for you is using personality tests. There are many different personality trait evaluations available, each with their own strategy for analyzing and interpreting your skill set and personality. But no matter which ones you take, they can all give you insight into how your mind and personality work.

Use personality tests to determine your own strengths. Many businesses will have all of their employees take a personality test to determine how to best leverage everyone's strengths, instead of simply trying to build on their weaknesses. For example, you may determine that the person in charge of customer support is not strong with empathy but is very detail minded. They may be better suited trouble-shooting problems than trying to work outside their skill set by dealing with angry customers.

Too often we try to fix our weaknesses rather than leverage our strengths. If you know what you are good at, play to those strengths and look for others who can complement your weaknesses. One great way to zero in on those strengths is through personality tests.

There are dozens of popular personality tests, and many of them have companion books that allow you to dive deep into your strongest traits. One of my favorites is *How the World Sees You* by Sally Hogshead. She breaks your traits down to your top two advantages and your one dormant advantage. Once you've taken the test, you get a great report that breaks out all the details, and I have to say, everyone that I have ever had take it agrees with their classifications.

If you want to do a quick personality test, 16Personalities is a great one you can take online in about five minutes. According to 16Personalities, I am a "Logician," which according to their explanation, is a pretty close match. Other tests worth looking into are the Myers-Briggs Type Indicator and the DISC assessment.

Now, everyone won't agree with everything on these tests, and over time our skills and personalities will change. But they may help you zero in on what you would be passionate about doing as a career, what environments help you to be most productive and creative, how you process information, and what management strategies you may find most effective for you. It is usually a good idea to jot down the outcomes of any tests that you take and list them on your résumé. This does two things: it shows the employer that you are serious about knowing your strengths, and it also allows them to adjust how they interview if that business uses a similar test.

IV. USING GOALS AND SELF-KNOWLEDGE TO START A CAREER PLAN

Of course, great company culture that fits your strengths and a rich environment that offers upward mobility can be found in almost any field. But don't start your career just anywhere.

Many students graduate with little knowledge of where they want their careers to go, even if they've been diligent about preparing their job-hunting strategies and know what kind of company environment they'd like to work in. Having a plan is so critical when making that first step of graduation; do not short-change yourself. Build a plan. Too often people take the first opportunity they are given, and five years later they realize their career path is at a dead end. The best cure for stalled careers is a plan that is periodically revisited monthly, quarterly, and annually.

Now, let's start with creating your career plan. This isn't a plan for ten years into your future—this is a plan for how to get you from college to that first great job that will launch your career.

Just like all great endeavors, your journey to the perfect career starts with a plan and goals, but not just any plan, probably the biggest plan you have ever created. Without a plan, you will just wander from job to job endlessly, hoping that each step is marginally better than the last. I see this happening far too often with young developers. You need to break that pattern by establishing a plan complete with your career goals and then executing that plan.

How often have you heard of someone building a career plan before graduation? Probably never, because it is extremely rare. Most college students have only one goal—graduate. That's an admirable goal, but a follow-up goal is just as important because a degree alone doesn't pay bills. And being underemployed with tens of thousands of dollars of debt is no way to start your career either.

The most successful career plans for college graduates require starting the plan a year or two before graduation. Yes, before graduation.

This section will briefly cover everything you need to build a custom career plan, and later chapters will tackle each of these elements in-depth. My planning will cover four critical steps necessary for the ideal career path:

Step 1: **Preparation.** Preparation includes obvious tasks like cleaning up your social media profiles and behaving professionally, but you also need to create and then build your personal brand with a website, content for a blog, and your professional portfolio. Remember, you can never be too prepared and you can never start planning too early.

Step 2: **Building a portfolio.** Building a comprehensive and active portfolio is better than showing years of experience on paper with just a computer science degree. Allowing a prospective employer to look at your actual development skills and validate your abilities for themselves is the best way to set yourself apart from the pack. Your degree means a lot of projects, skills, and experience, so that needs to be shown in your portfolio rather than only stated as a degree on your résumé. And if your portfolio reflects your personality, strengths, and goals, you'll be steps ahead.

Step 3: **Experience.** Since you probably have never worked professionally as a developer, you can only show your college course work as your experience. Unfortunately, every other graduating student has the exact same experience as you. Building additional experience is critical to set you apart from the pack. There's a lot you can do right now and in the immediate future to expand your experience and show your future employers how your experience stands out. If your experience shows your strengths, ambition, and focus, they'll take notice.

Step 4: **Interviewing.** Having a calculated plan for interviewing is critical to getting hired. Everything else is irrelevant if you cannot articulate and communicate your skills, knowledge, experience, and portfolio during an interview. I will give you guidance on how to nail your interview and what to avoid, and how to show them what they're looking for. (Hint: be yourself!) Knowing your goals and yourself well during the interview will demonstrate to them how much you value yourself.

We are going to walk through each of these steps and outline strategies for success in detail in later chapters, but each of these elements should be tackled as part of your career plan. It will take time and effort, but that extra effort now will be the difference between you and the average college graduate.

V. CAREER PLAN TEMPLATE

This template is designed to help you define the characteristics that you are seeking in your dream job. There are no right or wrong answers, because each question is just meant to help you think about your passions.

First, review this chapter and then fill out the questions below, thinking about your strengths, weaknesses, personality, desired career path, and the company culture that would be most rewarding for you.

Then, revisit this list and your answers with every company that you interview for, and evaluate whether that company meets your desired life goals.

CAREER QUESTIONNAIRE

My ideal career would be:

My first ideal job title would be:

My career goal for the next twelve months is:

My five-year career plans are:

The top five characteristics that I look for in a company are:

The top three characteristics that would prevent me from joining a company are:

At the end of my first three months, I want to have accomplished:

At the end of my first year, I want to have accomplished:

My desired relationship with my coworkers would be described as:

Amount of additional work am I willing to do to get ahead:

The company's culture must be like:

3

PREPARING FOR THE JOB HUNT
& BUILDING A PERSONAL BRAND

The very first step to building a solid career plan is making sure it's built on a good foundation. If you think you can get a job by just sending in a résumé and showing up for an interview, you are dead wrong. You need to prepare both yourself and how the world sees you before you ever submit a résumé. You must set yourself apart from the pack; the only way to do that is to prepare in advance and anticipate how your future employer will perceive you.

This preparation must be completed in advance of any résumé creation or any outreaches to prospective employers. You only get one chance to make a first impression—people have probably told you that all of your life, but have you ever really considered what it means? I recommend you start preparing at least one year before you graduate to allow your personal branding to have a good history. If your entire brand is built in a weekend, it will be obvious you just slammed it together and the effort will not appear genuine. The ultimate effect will reflect poorly on you.

When I first launched South Dakota Geeks, I had a college student who was about to graduate reach out to me ask if he could help coordinate events. He also wanted the opportunity to speak at an event about a side project he was working on. As a college student, he was able to present on a technical topic to a group of about forty other geeks around the city and have immediate credibility with each of them. He established his brand and credibility before he ever sat down for an interview with any of those businesses. By the time he graduated, he had multiple businesses that he was talking with and was able to secure a job that provided him with the culture, mentorship, and growth that he wanted. I still talk with him periodically, and I can't convince him to leave that company either.

I. PERSONAL BRANDING

Everyone has a personal brand; it is not something you can buy or license. You already have a personal brand, whether you know it or not. Your personal brand is the impression that people get about you, how you present yourself, and the words associated with you by others. People who identify and work to build a consistent brand are more focused and consistent with their communication. This consistent message will prove valuable while job seeking, networking, and interviewing.

Having a brand does not require an expensive logo or unique website design. It simply means your message, image, and the adjectives associated with you in people's minds are consistent and accurate. Your brand is about the impressions and expectations of you, your work, and your attitude.

Your brand must match your message. If you want to be known as someone who is always innovative and one step ahead of the curve, keep your innovation front and center with your actions. You want to always be talking about bleeding edge, unproven, and even risky technologies. You will not want to talk about boring, tried-and-true mainstream technologies, because those do not reflect your innovative brand.

An innovative brand requires excellent communication skills, because you will always be talking about technologies no one else is using.

The best way to discover and then build your personal brand is to first write down your true passions, then write down how you want people to see you. It's that simple.

Take a moment to stop reading now and write down both of those things. Put some time and reflection into it—the more focused and accurate it is, the more helpful it will be.

When you're done, use these two lists as a guide for all you do as you build your brand, and use them as a source of inspiration for what to write about on your blog.

This chapter includes a simple personal brand worksheet you should complete and use as well as a list of words you wish to resonate with those you meet. You should constantly be comparing your list of words to your messaging (actions, portfolio, online presence) to make sure they coincide with how you want your personal brand to be perceived by others. If your words and content don't match, you need to adjust your messaging. Your personal brand will likely change over time as you grow, so it is best to revisit this exercise periodically, at least once per year.

Since you are seeking a well-paid career as a developer, I would suggest your personal brand be something that reflects you as a person, your current experience, and your passions. This should be light, fun, energetic, young, motivated, ready to learn, and positive. It should not be dark, boring, lazy, unexciting, old, know-it-all, or negative—who would want to hire that person?

Your personal brand is you. Take your personal brand seriously and reflect on it with every project you choose, every blog post you write, and every meeting you attend. You should be the authentic you at all times. However, if the authentic you is someone unemployable or less desirable to employers, you must decide how to adjust your personal brand to be more aligned with who you want to be.

I see hundreds of college graduates who don't understand how much their negative personal brand affects their chances of early success. You can, and should, build your personal brand to reflect someone who will be motivated to grow and work hard to achieve great success.

II. PERSONAL BRAND TEMPLATE

Your personal brand is who you are, what you stand for, and how you want to be seen by the world. It summarizes you; it is your essence. You have a personal brand, whether you have defined it or not. By performing the following branding exercise, you can better understand who you are and adjust how you want to be perceived by your actions. Sometimes we need to be reminded about how our behavior affects how others see us.

This branding exercise focuses only on you and your job search; it does not dive deep into your core essence or mission. It's a great place to start, though, so grab a pencil and challenge yourself with these questions:

List the top five qualities that you want people to use when describing you:

In one sentence, describe how you would like to be introduced to a peer group:

Outline your work experience in 50–100 words:

Write a short bio of who you are in 50–75 words:

Write a full bio of who you are, using 200–300 words:

Describe your passion statement—what is it that makes you get up every day:

What are your five traits that you project each day?

What are the five action words that describe you?

This is the start of your personal brand. Once you have decided on your personal brand, think about how that brand would look on a website template, in a logo, for colors, and for content. You should document these thoughts so they can be reviewed periodically to make sure your work is properly representing your brand.

Make notes here on the tone and style of your brand (colors, website look, logo, etc):

It is rare to see someone with a computer science degree who understands their personal brand and puts it to work for them daily. This can be a huge opportunity for you to set yourself apart from the pack. Everything I cover in this book is designed to build an excellent personal brand—separate yourself!

As you build your website, portfolio, social media presence, and projects, follow your personal brand in everything you do.

III. SOCIAL MEDIA AS ONLINE BRANDING

In today's super-competitive job market, employers look for any reason to drop a candidate from consideration. One of the easiest ways to judge a candidate early in the process is to review their social media profiles. You may receive conflicting information about social media, but rest assured that any company worth working for will use every resource possible to evaluate candidates. This includes investigating your online presence, conducting background checks, and checking with your friends, professors, and colleagues. It has never been easier to look up information about a candidate online than it is now.

Long before you submit your résumé for that dream career, you must review all of your social media profiles and make them both professional and consistent with your brand. Depending on how prolific your usage of social media has been up until this point in time, this may actually take a while, so plan ahead. Alternatively, you can simply delete everything and start with a new, professional social image and brand. The choice is yours.

In a later chapter, under "Building Your Portfolio," I will cover how to leverage social media platforms in your favor by building a personal brand. But for now, you should make sure nothing problematic or immature that could prevent you from landing an interview in the future appears on any of your social media channels.

The most complex social media platform to manage is Facebook. Facebook not only holds what you post but also holds everything that anyone else posts about you. As a college student, you probably know what I am talking about. Make sure you look at all photos you were tagged in, as well as those you posted.

I had a current college student apply for an internship and it was a year when there were far more jobs than candidates, so I didn't receive many résumés. Out of the few that were submitted, one candidate stood out as a front-runner so I pulled up his Facebook page. Most of his pictures, more than 90% of them, were of him drinking beer or partying. Since he looked good on paper, I called him in for an interview anyway. If nothing else, I could explain to him that if he wanted to get a job, he needed to clean up his online profile. After a brief interview,

I brought up that I looked at his online profile. At first he didn't think anything about it until I mentioned that it was all inappropriate for someone looking for a job, and that I'm not the only one who will look. Just to see if he took my advice, I looked again the next day and sure enough, he took my advice and cleaned up all of his pictures. I ended up not hiring him or any candidates that year, but I suspect he nailed his next interview.

To secure and polish your online brand, complete the following four steps today:

Step 1: Lock down your Facebook profile so your information is more difficult to view and to prevent others from tagging you. Facebook has several security settings and they change frequently. In general, you want to set your profile to private and disable any friends-of-friends from being able to view your posts. It is also wise to not allow others to tag you in their photos without your approval.

This step will not prevent anyone from viewing your profile, but it will limit your exposure. I will cover how to leverage Facebook for networking later, but for now, you should keep it locked down.

Step 2: Review at least your last hundred posts on each social platform to see if anything could be taken out of context or represents you poorly. Anything questionable should be deleted. Deleting posts may not make them completely disappear, but it's a start. Take a look at all photos you have posted or in which you have been tagged. Delete the inappropriate photos and remove the tags.

Step 3: It is very easy for someone to see who you are friends with on most platforms, even if your profile is private. A lot can be said about you from those with whom you associate—remember that you are the average of the five people you hang around. Friends posting content which would reflect on you poorly should be unfriended or unfollowed.

Step 4: For each social platform you use, log out and then look at your profile like a prospective employer will be doing. Make sure the information showing up is accurate, clean, and in alignment with your personal brand. You may be surprised at how the world sees you; now is the time to clean up that view.

Now that I have your social media profiles under control, let's see what the rest of the world has to say about you. Using all top search engines, especially Google, search for yourself using your full name and any variations that a prospective employer might use. Hopefully not much comes back, especially since you are just starting your career and should not have a significant online footprint. Review at least the top two or three pages of results, even if they are not actually referring to you. You need to know what an employer will see.

If you are unfortunate enough to have a similar name as someone who has a negative online profile, don't panic. Now you know, and the easiest solution to this problem is to use a more unique version of your name as part of your online portfolio and brand. Options could be to use your middle initial or your full middle name. Make sure it gets used consistently, everywhere—your website, social media profiles, résumé, and everything else. It is not difficult to brand yourself at this point in your career; use this to your advantage.

While this is not likely going to be the case for you since I have already covered the value of having an online profile, I have run into candidates who have no online profiles at all. None, not a single one. This is also not a good idea, since virtually every business will attempt to locate you online, and finding no profile will raise its own red flags. Maybe you have no social life, maybe you don't understand rudimentary technology, maybe it incorrectly indicates your age. I'm not advocating that you need a profile on every platform, but prospective employers should be able to at least locate something about you online, especially if you are going to be working as a state-of-the-art developer at a high-tech company.

Now that your social media profiles are cleaned up, I can move on to building a website and blog as part of your portfolio and your online brand.

IV. CREATING A WEBSITE AND BLOG

All developers should have their own personal website to demonstrate their portfolio and build a personal brand. First, let's focus on why you need a website. You may be thinking blogs and websites are a thing of the past, and your brand is built around social media profiles. But blogging is still very popular and allows you to build a brand and image that you want future employers to find and judge you by.

Everyone should have a personal website because they are quickly replacing the traditional paper résumé. Remember, you want to set yourself apart from the pack. Does a one-page résumé show the breadth of your experience, skills, and portfolio? I sure hope it does not. You are a multidimensional entity; let your portfolio reflect all that you are professionally. A résumé is still important, because many businesses require them as the entry point for a job application. Think of your résumé as a lead-generator to your website. Use your résumé to push prospective employers to your personal website so they get the full experience of you and your brand. That's much more than you can do on a single piece of paper.

Your website shouldn't be complicated. All you need is a few pages that outline your experience, demonstrate your portfolio, and provide an interactive résumé. It should be ten web pages at the most, including a blog. Blogs may sound like an outdated technology, but they provide three crucial assets:

1. A blog demonstrates your ability to write and communicate.
2. A blog allows you to drive portfolio content, experiences, and skills to a prospective employer.
3. Search engines provide preferential treatment to blogs, so it allows you to push employers who search for you directly to your brand.

Building a website has never been easier. Remember, you are seeking a developer position so you must be able to accomplish the relatively simple task of building a WordPress site. I recommend using an inexpensive hosted WordPress platform instead of building your own from scratch, as tempting as that may be for a new developer. Launching a WordPress site is not the key skill you are demonstrating to a prospective employer; you are demonstrating why you built a website and how that experience is valuable.

Pick a WordPress or other content management system (CMS) platform and start with a clean theme to build your website. Add features that are unique and business-centric to demonstrate your web development skills. Focus on the latest visualizations, stylesheets, widgets, and extensions. Look at the websites of businesses with which you would like to interview, analyze the technologies they use, learn them, and implement them on your personal website.

If you want to pursue a more traditional development job that does not involve web front-ends, consider using a simple platform with standard templates, and focus your efforts on blogging about technology platforms that you find interesting. If becoming a database administrator is more in-line with your interests, develop a scale test suite and blog about the optimization you made. Always keep your dream-career goals and relevant technologies in mind when brainstorming content for your website.

Still confused on how to start building a personal website? Now is an excellent time to use those research skills your prospective employer will be looking for and go figure it out. Start by searching tutorials on Google and YouTube, locate a WordPress hosting company, and get to work. This will be the first item you add to your portfolio, not to mention it makes an excellent first blog post—"How I Created My Blog to Build My Portfolio."

Following and applying the discussion points of this chapter will make sure your online brand is consistent, professional, and an asset to you rather than a liability.

4

GAINING EXPERIENCE

Many college graduates don't have much experience in their career field that they can put on a résumé, which puts them at a huge disadvantage when it comes to finding a job. However, there are several strategies you can use to build that experience right now and set you apart.

Building real-world experience will take time and planning. I am going to cover how to obtain experience and build a portfolio before you graduate so that you increase your chances of lining up a well-paying career before graduation.

Without any job experience, you are at a disadvantage entering the job market as a software developer. The chances of landing your dream job are substantially better when you can demonstrate to a prospective employer you have mastered the skills involved with completing a project while writing good code.

There are many ways you can gain experience and build your portfolio; doing so is a must for every new software developer entering the job market today. Even experienced developers need to be able to demonstrate their skills through an updated portfolio.

New graduates need to have job-relevant experience when interviewing, because experience at the local fast food restaurant is not going to impress those conducting an interview. I am not saying that you cannot work during your college years, and in fact I think you should, because it builds accountability and shows your ability to actually show up at work every day of the week. I'm also not saying that you must have career-relevant experience in your portfolio in order to land a good first job out of college. But if you can gain it, it will set you apart.

Every graduating student does have experience—education. The problem with this experience is that every other graduating student has the same experience. For the most part, they all took the same classes, they all participated in the same projects, and they all have references from the same professors. Your goal is to set yourself apart from that pack of students with better, real-world experience that will resonate with prospective employers. The bar set by most college students is pretty low, so this works in your favor. Take advantage of this situation by putting in some hard work early on.

As you gain real-world experience and add it to your portfolio, make sure you always describe that experience in a way that is relevant to your new career. On both your résumé and your personal website, add a section that outlines your relevant work experience to showcase your experience to a prospective employer. A simple outline with bullet lists of how each job or project expanded your abilities in your specific topic has more value than listing the job itself. Do not forget to include school projects, pointing out the value you brought to each project. Avoid making references to "we," since it demonstrates that you were only a small player in the project.

Take a moment to list the major projects and skill-building assignments you've participated in for your degree so far that have helped make you a good software engineer. Jot down your role, the skills that role built for you, and how this relates to your career goals. Then add that content to your résumé. A résumé structure that will make this easier is the experience-focused résumé, examples of which you can find online. Your university will likely also have resources for helping you actually write and revise your résumé.

Now, let's cover how you gain valuable work-related experience to build a portfolio that will impress a prospective employer. There are several strategies you can use to build that experience. As someone who has interviewed hundreds of students over the years, I can safely report that very few will have any of these experiences upon graduation. This will set you apart from the pack in a way that will allow you to entertain multiple job offers and in some cases, write your own job offer to a company of your choice.

I. INTERNSHIPS

Every graduating senior should have completed an internship during college. There is no better experience to show than an internship; however, you probably will not learn much from the experience. Whether it is paid or unpaid, having an internship shows future employers two things: 1) you can show up for work on a regular basis and 2) you have enough ambition to actually seek out and complete an internship. Both are huge for a prospective employer.

Internships as a whole are largely flawed in most colleges and universities, but it is not their fault. In a career like software development, it takes a junior developer (someone with less than five years of experience) at least six months to come up to speed with the company's software to be efficient. How could you expect someone with zero experience (a college student) to add any value in a time period of eight to twelve weeks, over a summer nonetheless? Add on top of that the fact that those who are supervising your internship have a full workload themselves and probably do not want to put effort into helping someone who will be gone in a few months anyway. So don't expect much guidance during your internship. Little knowledge is gained from most internships, other than learning company culture, workplace etiquette, and perhaps some general systems and patterns of workplaces in your career field—but my points are still valid. You need to seek out and complete at least one internship during your college years. There are usually a few businesses that have good intern programs that have been refined over the years, and you should seek out and land one or more of those internships.

The best way to get value from an internship is to plan your internships early. Scout out job fairs during your first few years of college and get to know the companies who run internship programs and the people who choose their interns. Talk to fellow students who are working at internships currently or have had them in the past. Find out which companies offer the best experience, because you do not want to get stuck in the mail room stuffing envelopes for twelve weeks. Focus on companies that take internships seriously and actually have an internship program with a track record of teaching and hiring students after graduation. Ask your instructors which companies have the best programs, and then focus only on those businesses. Your time is valuable, so do not waste it on a bad internship experience.

Take the opportunity to do as many internships as possible. Even short internships over Christmas breaks are valuable if they're done at the right businesses. Plan on doing two or three internships throughout your four years at college. The more experience you have at graduation, the more attractive you will be to future employers. Multiple internships will also help build your social network. Many companies have internship programs for the sole purpose of hiring the best students after graduation, so make sure they seek you as a future employee.

During your internship, make sure you put in the best effort you can with every task you are given. This is your opportunity to demonstrate your skills, but more importantly, your work ethic and attitude. You may never work for the company after your internship ends, but your success will likely travel to other companies quickly. You will likely end up asking your supervisor for recommendations as well, and a great recommendation from a leading local business can be incredibly valuable. Make sure you show up on time every day, work hard at every task, ask good questions, and keep a positive attitude, even if the tasks are not challenging. Always ask for more work and more responsibility, because the worst they will say is no.

After you complete your internship, send a follow-up thank-you card to those in charge of the program and your supervisors. Ask them if you can use them as business references for future job interviews. Now would also be a great time to ask for a letter of recommendation that you can use in your portfolio. You will have better luck getting a letter of recommendation if you send them a draft version that they can simply edit and sign.

Keep in mind that the work done during an internship probably will be confidential and you may not be able to share what you did during future interviews. Be sure to clear up exactly what you can and cannot talk about before you complete your internship program. Larger companies will likely perform an exit interview, which is the perfect place to clarify these details. Don't be afraid to ask; it will prevent a potential issue in the future.

To summarize:

- Plan on doing two or more internships throughout your college career. Focus on key businesses that have the best internship programs in your area and have a track record of hiring full-time employees out of their internship candidates.
- Networking is a very important part of internships, so use your time to be efficient and meet as many influential people within the organization as you can.
- *Work hard, show up on time, and treat your internship as a real job, not as a temp job that you cannot wait to leave.*

- Ask questions and learn as much as you can during your internship program. Become a great student and prospective employee.

II. CODE BOOT CAMPS

One emerging trend in our nation today is code boot camps. A code boot camp is like a well-organized internship where you can learn real-world development skills, along with valuable soft-skills which are not always taught in traditional education settings. Typically, a code boot camp will be eight to twelve weeks long and will be an all-day learning experience. Good boot camps will be servicing a niche skill set in high demand within their community and will help you build a targeted portfolio. Since code boot camps have limited timespan, typically only a few months, they will focus on one key development area, like Ruby on Rails or user interfaces or WordPress.

Typically, there are three key areas where code boot camps will accelerate your career choices:

1) Vertical specific knowledge.
2) Networking opportunities with prospective employers.
3) Building a portfolio consisting of real-world experience.

Since the job market for entry-level developers is extremely competitive, any way that you can set yourself apart from the crowd gives you a huge advantage. If you have an opportunity to add a code boot camp experience to your résumé, it may be the single most valuable advantage that you can have over every other candidate.

Code boot camps focus intensely on one language or platform, usually a platform that is readily used within the community that they serve. This vertical specific knowledge will provide you an advantage over those who have only a general-level knowledge, which is typically taught at traditional colleges. Code boot camps will also focus heavily on job placement, and they will go to great lengths to line up the appropriate business sponsors who require these skills, even sometimes providing a private job fair.

This book has an entire chapter dedicated to networking because it is such an important part of your ability to land an interview and pursue your desired career. Businesses will pay thousands of dollars to have a chance to meet all of the boot camp participants and to interview them one-on-one before the boot camp concludes. This is a great networking opportunity to take advantage of as someone who is getting started out in their career.

Code boot camps will give you an advantage that you cannot obtain otherwise. You will be expected to pay a fee to attend a boot camp, and depending on your community, the fees will vary significantly from a few thousand dollars to tens of thousands of dollars. But if you compare that to adding another year of college, or if it makes the difference of having your dream job versus just a job, the benefits far outweigh the costs.

This book is dedicated to building a thorough portfolio for you to use when landing your perfect career, and code boot camps will put you in front of the right projects for your portfolio. Work projects will be hand-picked to best leverage the curriculum being taught, and the sponsors who are looking to hire the graduates. Unlike "busy-work" projects that are often part of college curriculums, boot camp projects will actually be used by businesses and referenceable by you during your upcoming interviews. Projects like these show your skills, set you apart, give you measurable experience, and further your brand.

To investigate boot camps in your area, use Bloc [https://www.bloc.io/learn-to-code/], which has an online index organized by location and boot camp type.

Now Go Execute

- Investigate whether your community has a code boot camp to attend.
- If you cannot afford to attend, ask if there are scholarship options or possibly ways to audit the program.

III. OPEN-SOURCE COMMUNITIES

Open-source software is software written by a community of developers and is typically licensed by those developers for use by anyone else to use or modify. Open-source projects account for some of the largest software projects around today, including web browsers, code frameworks, office suites, web servers, and operating systems. Anyone can contribute to these projects, although large projects have very strict standards and policies in place, and may not accept your contributions.

GitHub is one of the largest repositories of open-source software projects. Another large community is operated though SourceForge. net. Both platforms have code repositories, bug tracking, and project planning tools built in for collaboration. GitHub typically only provides raw code, while SourceForge also often includes the compiled binaries for many projects.

To build credibility as a developer, you should contribute to one or more open-source projects in your free time. You don't need to write a kernel component either. Many open-source projects need developers to work on documentation, installation scripts, test suites, and quality-control testing. These are great ways to get involved with limited time commitment but still build a reputation within the respective communities, your résumé, and your experience.

Other great roles for new developers are helping manage a project's message boards and helping with project management, test suites, sample code, debugging, and beta testing. Very little development experience is necessary for these roles, but they are critical for every project. What better way to learn a project than to be one of their beta testers who helps identify and fix bugs?

Picking projects that you are passionate about will help keep you motivated. Also avoid working on projects that do not have any recent activity, since you may get stuck without any support from a team leader. There are millions to choose from, so you should not have a problem finding something that you want to work on. Take ownership and treat the project with respect and care like you would your own project.

Find a few projects to which you want to contribute, and then start to contribute. There is no reason not to, and you may even get noticed by the project owners and may be asked to join their team as a leader. Being able to put your name to a community GitHub project will validate your portfolio for any prospective employer. Many times, these open-source projects are themselves commercially backed. Who knows, you may even get an opportunity to work for them as your full-time day job.

Now Go Execute

- Pick one or two open-source projects that you are passionate about and start contributing. Join their newsletters and message boards, and start interacting with them.
- Learn as much as you can about the projects that you choose, and treat them with respect as you would if they were your own projects.
- Add these projects to your portfolio on a personal website. If possible, link directly to your contributions along with a description of what you contributed to the project.

- If you see a gap in support, testing, documentation, or features, just jump right in and contribute. Ask if you can be the lead on a feature, bug, or task. There are plenty of jobs and tasks to go around.
- Be professional, authentic and genuine. Don't overcommit to things you will not be able to accomplish, and take small steps at the beginning. Remember, you are playing with some very senior engineers in these communities.

IV. MORE ABOUT GITHUB

GitHub (http://GitHub.com) is a git platform where anyone can post their code for anyone else to view, modify, and use. Everything posted to GitHub, in general, is open-source and available for others to contribute to, unless you choose to do a private repository. GitHub is primarily two things: a git version control platform and a large open-source code community. There are millions of code repositories hosted by GitHub, including some of the biggest frameworks in use today. GitHub has changed how open-source projects are operated and has opened up the opportunity for anyone to have their own code repository for free.

Every developer entering the job market should have an active GitHub account. One great thing about GitHub is that it shows your activity over time, as well as your project's activity. As a job seeker, it will be valuable to demonstrate an active GitHub account when a prospective employer looks at your account.

There are two ways that you need to use GitHub in your portfolio: 1) as *your* code repository and 2) to contribute to an open-source code project.

As you build your portfolio of code, I suggest that you submit your projects into GitHub for prospective employees to view. By default, everything will be open to the public, so keep that in mind if you are working on a shared project or a project that you would rather not make public. If you want to save code privately in GitHub, they provide private git repositories for a few dollars per month. Your GitHub activity shows both your public and private activity, so if you do keep some of your active projects private, your account will still show your activity.

I recommend that you push all of your code into GitHub. Keep it well documented and well organized since you will be encouraging prospective employers to review your work. Even if your projects are not standalone, you should check them in anyway. Prospective employers are not going to be downloading and looking at your code as a project but rather reviewing how your code looks—is it logically laid out and well commented, does it follow coding standards, is it clear and concise and containing everything else that an experienced developer would do? Use this opportunity to put your best foot forward by adding documentation, a "readme.md" file, test suites, and the appropriate amount of logic to every project.

The second way that you want to leverage GitHub is to fork an existing project and be active in an open-source community. When you fork a project, you essentially make your own copy of the project into your own GitHub account which can then be modified without impacting the original version. Forking a project instead of just copying it allows you to push your changes back to the original project and pull project updates into your version in the future. Forking also allows you to do your own things without getting permission from the original author. Keep in mind that there may be licensing restrictions on what you can and cannot do with projects that you fork.

While building your portfolio, you should identify a few open-source projects that you are passionate about and contribute actively to those projects. You may think that an entry-level developer with no experience could not possibly contribute to an open-source project, but that is not the case. There are many other ways to contribute.

In addition to GitHub, there are other code repositories as well, such as Bitbucket and SourceForge. Keep your eyes open for the right project, not the right distribution platform.

I love GitHub as a way to demonstrate your experience, and I use it for absolutely everything. I keep a lot of old code snippets in mine, because you never know when they might be valuable to someone else. I hope that in the near future I can have job candidates submit their GitHub profile name instead of a résumé.

Now Go Execute

- Create a GitHub account, set up your profile, download the GitHub scripts, and begin to check in your portfolio projects.
- Any work that you do for yourself, including modifications to WordPress plugins and themes, should be pushed into your GitHub repository as long as it does not violate the original author's licensing restrictions.
- Follow the original author's conventions and road map if you want to be able to push your modifications back into the original code base.
- Treat GitHub as one of your social media platforms: be active and join the communities.

V. NONPROFIT WORK

Every community has a ton of nonprofits that rely on volunteers to meet their missions. A great way to build a portfolio is to volunteer your technical skills to these nonprofits. You can offer to update or build them a new website, optimize their technology infrastructure, provide their board training, or pretty much anything else that they need done.

Listing volunteer work on your résumé is always a plus, but listing that you volunteered your professional skills is even better. Not only does it speak to your character and your personal brand, it provides a way for prospective employers to see your work for themselves.

The easiest ways to contribute your skills is to build a new website for a nonprofit. For all the same reasons that you should have a personal website, every nonprofit can benefit from the same advice. Nonprofits are often stuck with poorly designed, poorly implemented, and poorly maintained websites which they cannot afford to maintain or update, leaving them stuck in the past.

Offer to migrate their existing website to an easier-to-use platform like WordPress. Start by setting up the initial content and then provide them with adequate training to maintain it themselves. This will help a great organization as well as add experiences to your portfolio—win-win. Leveraging a platform like WordPress will also allow them to take over the content themselves with little training, so you will not be on the hook making changes for years to come.

Make sure you provide them with all of the details such as where it is hosted, login credentials, renewal dates, domain name registration, and an update plan. Put all of this information into a single document that they can print, store, and reference in the future. Make sure you include everything that the next developer would need to pick up where you left off, since you might not be there in the future.

Another suggestion is to build an event website for a nonprofit. Most nonprofits host annual fundraisers but rarely have the resources to build an event-specific website. An event website may only be needed for a few months, which means you will not be responsible for any long-term maintenance or questions. Sites like Strikingly and SquareSpace are great ways to set up simple sites for short periods of time.

Finding a nonprofit to contribute to can also be a fun project in itself. There are many ways this can be done. Start by picking something that you are passionate about, do some research, ask friends and family, or check out your state's Secretary of State website or national nonprofit registries, and then send them an e-mail or stop by the nonprofit's office. Don't hesitate to ask them how you can help out. They may have technical struggles that you can easily solve without writing any code.

Keep in mind your personal brand, and bring that brand into your decision as well. Only work on projects that you are passionate about; otherwise you will quickly become resentful of the time you are spending on the project. Resentment is the fastest way to sour a great relationship.

Be careful that you do not overcommit, which is very easy to do with nonprofits. Only take on projects that you know you can accomplish. If you do set up a website, make sure you thoroughly document everything for them, including the login and password information.

Ask them if they would allow you to put a note on the website saying that you donated your time and experience. This will further solidify your credibility with your portfolio. Make sure you add all the work to your portfolio website as well. Also ask them for a letter of recommendation, which will prove to be valuable later when you interview for your first job.

Now Go Execute

- Everyone should contribute to at least one nonprofit. Your commitment may be a few hours per month, but the benefits are enormous.
- Be honest and genuine with what you can actually contribute. Never overcommit, because even though you are volunteering, no one wants someone who does not follow through with their commitments.
- Continue your nonprofit philanthropy throughout your career. The work is very rewarding and offers a unique networking experience as you grow your career.

VI. FREE WEB WORK

In addition to nonprofits, many small businesses cannot afford to create an elaborate website and often get stuck with a simple, single-page website hanging out there on an unknown platform. Often, they will not even remember that they have a website or their login or how to update the content.

A great way to build your portfolio is to offer to do free work for a local business, especially one that you have some connection or relationship with. Consider approaching your favorite restaurant, coffee shop, property management company, or even comic book store with an offer to build them a new website in exchange for a letter of recommendation. Building a personal relationship is also a great way to network with businesses that may be able to make a valuable connection for you in the future through a personal introduction. It can be difficult getting started with freelance work, but by strategically offering free work, you may be able to build a small side business while also developing your own work portfolio.

Unlike working with a nonprofit organization, a local business may not be as willing to have just anyone build them a website, especially if you do not have any references. Start by explaining that you are a recent college graduate who is seeking a job as a developer and that you are building a work portfolio. Ask the business if they would be interested in having a new website design for a low cost and then provide them with a very specific plan. While you may be willing to do the work for free, you may want to first ask for a minimum fee to cover your expenses. After all, your time does have a value, even if you are just getting started.

Remember not to overcommit your skills or time here either. If you end up not being able to finish the project, it may come back to you in a negative way. If the work is beyond your comfort zone or skills, do not commit to doing the work. Politely explain that your skills are not refined enough at this time to do a sufficient job and pass on the project. It is always better to pass on a project than take it and fail to complete it.

Upon completion, ask for a letter of recommendation. Provide them with a draft letter that is easy for them to modify instead of asking them to write you one from scratch. Most people are happy to provide an honest recommendation as long as it does not require from them too much time. They often don't know how to write a recommendation, either, so providing a draft will ensure a better outcome. Also ask them if you could add a "built by" message on their website to help build your portfolio and credibility. Always make it easy for them to recommend your services to others as well.

Another strategy to pursue would be to actually build a business a new website before you approach them with an offer. Explain that you needed the practice anyway so you took a chance and built them a new website. You may not want to ask for any money for them to use the new website, but instead ask for a reference and introductions to other businesses who could use your services.

Rarely, you may find yourself doing some free freelance work for someone who is just completely unreasonable. They may be abusive, dismissive, demanding, or just outright difficult to work with. This can put you in a bind because they are also the ones who are most likely to complain to everyone about how your work wasn't up to their standards. At all costs, try to avoid working with these difficult people, but if you find out too late, there is always hope. Simply suggest that you are not the right person for the job and that you are not able to continue to help them. If they did pay you anything, make sure you reimburse them the full amount as well, which can be tricky. Never get into an argument with them, because it only ends badly for you, even if you are right.

Now Go Execute

- Offer free or low-cost services to local businesses to build experience and expand your network.

- When offering free or discounted work, the work needs to be beneficial to you and the business. Websites are great projects because they can easily be added to your portfolio and reviewed by future employers.
- Target businesses that you have an existing relationship with or have an interest in working with. People are more willing to work with you if they have a personal connection.
- Always ask for a letter of recommendation, especially if the work is free or very low cost. But provide them with a draft recommendation letter that they can easily customize.

VII. START YOUR OWN COMPANY

I'm not recommending that every college student create their own business; however, it may be something that is right for you. Building a business takes a real commitment and many will fail before they get enough work to cover the costs of setting up the entity. However, for some of you, this may be the perfect solution, especially if you are planning on building a freelance business after college.

Creating a legal entity to operate as a business can be complex, with many ramifications that you may not see initially but still could cost you a ton of money in the future. There is one thing that you absolutely must keep in mind when you charge anyone to do work—taxes. Uncle Sam wants his share, and he will spend thousands of dollars to collect a few hundred dollars from you, so do not skip paying taxes! This includes federal, state, local, and sales taxes. Of course, many vary by state so you will need someone who can guide you. Not doing this is the number-one mistake made by new business owners.

In general, there are only two types of businesses you need to consider when getting established; you will either be a sole proprietorship or limited liability company (LLC). I will not go into a lot of detail on these, but in general, an LLC is registered with a state as a business and provides additional legal protection for the owners (you) while a sole proprietor is anyone who is operating a business but is not registered as a corporation. As a sole proprietor, you can be sued and you are personally liable for your actions, although the LLC doesn't provide a ton of extra protection.

If you do decide to form an LLC, you can do it yourself for less than two hundred dollars or pay an attorney about a thousand dollars to do it for you. The process is not very complicated, but you must file annual reports and some states will require corporate bylaws to be submitted. Setting up an LLC is not the same as paying taxes or registering with the IRS, so do not confuse the two.

In general, you should start a sole proprietorship because you don't need to do anything except act like a business. All of your income will be taxed as your personal income, both for federal and state taxes, and don't forget about sales tax either.

In all cases, you must pay federal income tax on all money earned. In general, you must submit quarterly reports and payments to the IRS, but this is very easy to do. If you live in a state that has a sales tax, you may also need to collect sales tax on all transactions. Make sure that you do not forget to collect the sales tax from your clients; otherwise, you will be paying out of your pocket. Sales tax is typically reported and paid monthly or quarterly, and your state will be more than helpful with setting up an account and helping you pay your taxes. Every state is different, so make sure you find someone who knows the right answers for your situation.

Another consideration for when you start a business is how you will manage your accounting books. Bookkeeping is not complicated; however, you may want to spend your time on other parts of your business where you can actually make money. Consider outsourcing your accounting and tax needs to the professionals. You may be surprised at how efficient you can be when someone else does these tasks for you, while avoiding mistakes that you will inevitably make the first time around.

Brand your business according to your goals, develop a logo with business cards, and write yourself a business summary. You should focus on only one type of development, such as websites for coffee shops, which will allow you to focus on that single niche area and eventually dominate that market in your community. Sure, you could create a website for anyone, but there are probably twenty other companies doing that well already. If you stay narrow and focused on one niche, you can focus on that industry's exact needs and build yourself a slight competitive advantage over the established companies in your market.

In addition to creating a website, logo, and business cards, consider how you want to advertise your services. Decide on how you will attract clients, how many projects you will take on at once, and how you will service clients over time. If your goal is to get a full-time day job eventually, make sure your clients do not expect you to be available during the day for calls or emergencies, or otherwise you will have some very unhappy clients or else an unhappy employer in the future.

Operating your own business can be very rewarding and freeing, but it also takes experience and hard work. I would recommend finding a business mentor who can help show you the ropes of being a small business owner in your community to avoid making mistakes. Start with the chamber of commerce or business incubator to locate a mentor. After all, there is no point in operating a business that will only lose money.

You may be able to partner with advertising agencies to pick up small projects that are too small for them to take on. Often they will work with various subcontractors for niche or small projects and then mark up your costs to their clients. This type of work is great because you will not be on the hook to do long-term maintenance, plus you can work with one client instead of many. The downside to working with an agency is that you will have little freedom on the projects, will literally be told exactly what you need to do, and must do it exactly as you're told.

There are a number of online sites that coordinate freelancers for hire. One of the biggest sites is Upwork (http://upwork.com), where you can post a profile and bid on projects. Upwork takes care of a lot of the details and risks when working with customers. When you're getting started, freelance sites are a great way to gain experience and build a business. Expect to work harder and get paid less than everyone else at the beginning, but for significant rewards and payoff later in your career.

Now Go Execute

- Freelancing is not for everyone, because you need to work with customers and sell yourself as a business owner. But consider whether it's a good fit for you.
- Do not forget about collecting or paying taxes!
- Getting started as a freelance business will be tough at first. Expect your first few projects to go horribly wrong, but learn from the experiences and adjust.

5

NETWORKING

I grew up in an average household in Hamilton, Montana. We weren't wealthy, but we weren't poor either. I started my first job when I was fourteen years old, changing irrigation pipe in alfalfa fields, and that is exactly as boring as it sounds. Twice a day, I trucked through a giant field and moved twenty-five-feet-long, aluminum irrigation pipes fifty feet over to water a different part of the field. I never hated it, because it was just something kids did where I grew up.

But that's not the job I want to talk about. The way I landed my second job is story-worthy. When I was a freshman in high school, the state changed their college entrance requirement to include Algebra II as a prerequisite. I was in the accelerated math track, so I was taking Algebra II as a freshman, and that year our school had about five freshmen and twenty seniors in that class. I was a shy kid and definitely one who would not fraternize with a senior. A senior named Stacy sat next to me that year, and she needed to pass to get into college.

Throughout the entire year, I helped her out more than our teacher did. I re-explained equations, provided her with better examples, walked her through the exercises, and acted as her personal Algebra II tutor in class. Our teacher was a great teacher, but Stacy just resonated with me better for some reason.

As school started to wrap up for the year, I was in search of a different job. Changing irrigation pipes was fine, but there was a cap on which you could earn—$0.10 per pipe, twice a day, for thirty-five sections, or seven dollars per day. Our town had the standard fast-food, retail, and labor jobs, which I was fine with, but I got word that the town laboratory had a few open positions for high school students on a work program, something that they had been doing for years. These were the "good" jobs for a high school kid. The pay was minimum wage ($3.15 an hour) but the work and experience were great. I rode my bike over to the laboratory after school and filled out the two-page application. They probably had fifteen or more applicants for the three open positions, so my chances were not good.

Unbeknownst to me, Stacy worked there and was leaving to head off to college. The laboratory left her in charge of selecting her replacement, and there was my application in the pile. She told her supervisor that I would be the best candidate for the job, she lined me up an interview, and I was hired on the spot because of her recommendation.

I continued to work there through my remaining high school years. If it weren't for that job, who knows what I would be doing today. Over the three years that I worked there, I learned how to program computers.

My job was exactly what you would think they would have an inexperienced high school kid do—wash equipment, stock shelves, and empty trash, just like every kid did before me.

Almost immediately after starting, I found a computer in a small back room that no one ever used. Until that moment, I hadn't given computers a second thought, because they simply didn't exist in my daily life. This was in the late '80s when no one had personal computers, and virtually no businesses had computers either. No one at the laboratory knew how to use it, and most of the scientists preferred slide rules over calculators anyway. During my downtime, which was about 80% of my time, I would plop down in this closet-room and just play around with that computer. They had an expensive database program called Paradox, but no one had any idea how to use it. I asked everyone there if they needed me to build them a database system, and eventually one of them said yes. They agreed to buy me the only published book for Paradox, and I set out to write my first program, with zero experience and no one to help me out.

This was the first computer that I had ever touched, no one in the entire facility knew how to write a program, and I was a freshman going on sophomore in high school. And this was the first computer I had ever laid my hands on.

During that summer, I read the entire Paradox book from cover to cover multiple times, taking it home to study every diagram and every line of example code. The exercises that they covered were not relevant to what I needed to do, so I had to figure out virtually everything myself. There was no Google, and in fact the Internet was Telnet and Gopher, so unless you wanted to know what the weather was outside, it was of no help. If a resource did exist to help me out, I didn't know how to find it.

By the time the summer was over, I had developed a database to store and organize all the cell samples that were stored in liquid nitrogen across multiple labs. All of their records were previously kept on graph paper in three-ring binders spanning more than ten years of research, where pages would frequently fall out, so this was a big improvement. The program also had data integrity checks, entry forms, backups, and even a search feature—something that the graph paper did not do well.

The program was amazing, but since no one in the laboratory knew how to turn on the computer, it actually never got used by anyone but me. They would leave notes on my desk asking me to look up cell locations and for new entries to record.

Over the next few years, I continued to expand the program and loved tinkering with the code. My passion for technology was known by everyone there, and my senior year of high school, one of the PhDs

I worked for asked me what I was going to do after I graduated. I didn't have a plan since I could not afford college, so she hooked me up with her husband, who did consulting for public utilities.

From there, I worked for him for just over a year before he merged with another larger company. After the merger, I went to work for the larger company in Washington, DC, for two years. He eventually left that organization to launch a technology startup company, and he asked me to join him as employee number one. That eventually led to BrightPlanet.

Networking alone won't build a successful career, but few successful careers develop without it. Skill, ambition, and hard work are absolutely necessary, but when you combine those with networking skills, you'll be able to write your own ticket to success.

I. STARTUP WEEKENDS

A great way to build experience and expand your network is to participate in local startup events, like Startup Weekend. Startup Weekend takes places all over the world, and they are very well-organized events, so find a local event to attend on their website (http://startupweekend.org/).

All Startup Weekend events are the same. They start with sixty-second pitches on Friday night, where anyone can pitch an idea. All the pitches are voted on and the top-voted ones are selected. Everyone self-selects into groups and then you spend the next fifty-three hours building a business around that idea, and many of them pivot from the original pitch. Come Sunday night, each team presents a five-minute pitch to a panel of judges who select the top three based on a number of criteria.

I have seen some businesses launch out of Startup Weekend pitches, but I've seen a lot more people land jobs, even if that wasn't their original goal for the weekend.

Over the years, I have led multiple teams during Startup Weekends. It's a lot of fun to take someone who has never launched a business before and go through the entire process with them over fifty-three hours. This is an experience that everyone should take advantage of. The costs are minimal but the value is immeasurable.

And if you do participate in events like this, be sure to add them to your résumé. It shows your ambition, your ability to work in teams, and your ability get in there to get the job done.

You can also pop into your local coworking space and ask them what entrepreneur events are occurring in your area. If the events are expensive to participate or join, ask them if there are any businesses that are offering to sponsor students to participate, because there usually are.

Events like these usually attract people who can help you build your career by teaching, connecting, and opening doors for you. During the events, make sure you take time to introduce yourself to everyone who is participating, every mentor who comes to help, each coordinator, and all of the business sponsors. Assume that each of them has a job waiting for you, and you just need to show them that you are the right candidate.

II. MENTORSHIP

When Josh Stroschein and I first started our discussions around launching Code Bootcamp, we felt strongly that every student needed to be exposed to senior developers as mentors. Why did we both feel so strongly about this?

One simple reason: it's hard getting started as an entry-level developer. And why doesn't everyone, regardless of their career, have a mentor to help build their craft? I can fix that for our Code Bootcamp students, so I made it a priority and part of our core goals for each class.

Here are four reasons why you should find a mentor in the software engineering field:

1.   A Sounding Board for the "New Guy."

The reason businesses hire a new developer is because their current development team has more work than they can handle. This causes a training issue for the business; how does the "new guy" get experience without derailing the existing development team? The answer is that they can't. That means every question, regardless of what it is, will take your experienced developer offline while he helps the new guy gain experience, which can cause frustration for everyone.

While mentors are not there to train you, they can be another sounding board for questions—especially those questions that may not get asked due to embarrassment or lack of confidence. Everyone can use a good friend to talk shop with, right?

2.   Guidance for the Beginners.

Development is a big world and it is growing every day. No one can know everything that is happening in every field of the industry. However, senior mentors have mastered ways to stay abreast through experience and networking. Being able to bounce ideas off an experienced mentor will help you avoid going down the wrong path. I have more than twenty years of experience and am learning new things every single day.

3.   Structured Networking for Introverts!

Networking is critical, especially for those who may sit at a desk all day long writing code or for those who might describe themselves as introverts. A mentor can be part of a structured relationship that is more comfortable and beneficial than a big networking event.

4. Everyone wins.

Everyone needs a mentor, regardless of the industry. Most successful people have a mentor with whom they can bounce ideas around, talk industry strategy, get help with complex questions, and further build a business network. Everyone wins!

Plus, those who have mentors early in their careers are more likely to be mentors later in life as well, further helping out the next generation of developers and completing the circle of knowledge. Every developer should have a strong support network.

My career was heavily influenced by mentors. Early in my career I was the one inexperienced developer among a small team of experienced developers, each passing on their advice to me. As I grew to be one of those experienced developers, I surrounded myself with other junior developers and took over the mentorship role. And I still have strong mentors today and I mentor many developers as well.

Many times people get too hung up on titles and try to formalize the mentor/mentee roles. This is not only unnecessary, it will actually get in the way of building a good relationship. People ask me how to find a mentor—but you don't, they find you. So how does someone get found by a mentor? By being there and asking the right questions.

The first step is to identify those who are at a point in their career that you want to be. If you want to be a great mobile phone developer, find someone who is a great mobile phone developer. Now, reach out to them and ask to set up a coffee or lunch. Today with social media, it has never been easier to get in contact with anyone, so send them a tweet or give them a call. There is a really good chance they will say yes to the opportunity.

Don't waste their time. Explain to them where you are in your career and the goals you have set for yourself. Take this opportunity to find out what they did to get to where they are today. Take notes, ask questions, and be appreciative of their time.

As long as you don't constantly bother them with trivial questions, they will probably be more than willing to help you accomplish your goals. Suggest a monthly coffee where you can share your progress and get their feedback. And don't be surprised if they start inviting you to events or if they ask you to help out on a project. Your ambition to reach out to a mentor says a lot about you; it sets you apart from the pack as being worthy of a challenge.

Also keep in mind, a mentorship can be as short as a one-time coffee or a one-day event, or as long as an entire career. The people I mentor sometimes only have short-term challenges that I can easily help them with, while other times I've followed them and their careers for years. Some were employees and others were just people I met at events. I have hired some and offered personal recommendations to others. Some have become business partners and lifelong friends.

Remember, someday you will be the mentor. Take on the job with pride. Perhaps you can start today by mentoring a first-year student at your college, or a local high school student. Regardless of where you are in your career, there is always someone else who is even newer than you.

III. MEETUPS AND DEVELOPER GROUPS

A great way to get plugged into the local developer community is to attend local Meetups in your community. Head over to Meetup.com and search your area, because they are usually free to attend.

In-person Meetups are great ways to make connections, talk with other developers, and even present your own ideas. Ask to speak at an upcoming event and spend time preparing a good presentation. It will make you an expert on that topic, even if you are not a true expert.

If your community doesn't have Meetups, you could always start one. Ask your local library or coffee shop if they would allow you to host your event at their location and start promoting it online. You will need to have an interesting topic to present at your first meeting, and the better prepared you are, the better luck you will have with getting a base set of attendees. It takes work running a group, but it will set you apart from the pack as the person who coordinated the developers' Meetup. Make sure you add it to your résumé as well.

A lot of development communities have also set up Slack user groups to communicate, discuss problems, and post job openings. Right now, there are no indexes of these groups, so your best bet is to attend local Meetups and ask around.

IV. USING SOCIAL MEDIA FOR NETWORKING

While I like to believe that books are never judged by their covers, it just isn't true. You will be judged by employers for everything you have done, including everything you have posted on social media. Social media has quickly become the single most valuable way an employer can look into your brand and personality before they ever call you in for an interview. In this section we are going to cover each of the popular social media platforms and explain how to best leverage each of them in your career journey.

LinkedIn

LinkedIn is the number-one professional social media site. They are often referred to as the social media platform for those looking for a job or looking for employees. LinkedIn is by far the most important social media platform for those looking for a job, especially in the software engineering field. *You must have a great LinkedIn profile.*

Long before your first interview, you need to make sure that you have a well-organized LinkedIn profile. This is actually very easy to do, because LinkedIn will walk you through the entire process and will continually prompt you about additional information to add based on the information you already gave, until your profile is complete—they even have a "percentage complete" bar to cheer you on.

Start with your education, past work experience, and a brief explanation of your skills and background. Make sure you use a professional-looking photograph for your avatar as well. You don't need to pay for a professional headshot, just make sure your photo is recent and shows a clear image of your face. And it shouldn't be one of you cropped out of a group photo, either!

Make sure that your LinkedIn profile is consistent with your personal brand and website, since the two will go hand-in-hand in telling prospective employers about why you make a great candidate. Here is an opportunity to talk about your portfolio work by including links to your personal website, blog, Twitter profile, GitHub account, and the projects you have worked on.

LinkedIn has a special section just for projects, so make sure you take advantage of this section by listing each project in detail. Do not list your projects as work experience because it will look like you have skipped from one job to another after only a few months, and that is just the wrong impression that you want to leave with prospective employers. Instead, list each as a project with an appropriate name, description and a link to where a prospective employer can view your work—this might be a website or GitHub account.

Genuinely connect with those whom you know within LinkedIn. LinkedIn will let you import your e-mail addresses of contacts to easily find connections. Connect with your professors, past employers, and colleagues, but avoid making connections to celebrities or political figures as it cheapens your profile quality and looks like you will connect with anyone just to increase your connection count. Remember, this is not Facebook, so avoid connecting with just friends and classmates. Be very strategic with your LinkedIn connections, and use it to show your circle of influences.

Before applying for any job, make sure you review their LinkedIn company profile, and it would be a good idea to "follow" them as well. This does two things: it shows you are genuinely interested in their company and it allows them to view your content since you are part of the same business circle. Only do this if you are comfortable with any of your connections knowing that you are somehow interested in that business.

You can make a request within LinkedIn for others to write you a LinkedIn recommendation. Send requests to your professors and ask them if they would write you a recommendation. This will show that they are more than just an acquaintance. Providing a reciprocal recommendation first might also encourage them to write you a recommendation.

Recommendations should be geared toward your experience and the skills that you want to promote. Take a look around LinkedIn to find what language others use in their recommendations and emulate the same tone and depth.

When at networking events, ask people for their business cards and then connect with them on LinkedIn afterwards. Send them a connection request within a day or two of the event, or otherwise they may not remember you. During the connection request, write a personal note like, "It was great to meet you yesterday at the [xx] social event. I look forward to chatting with you again next time." This is also a great time to make a follow-up request for coffee or lunch if they are someone you feel can help you out with your job search.

Join appropriate LinkedIn groups which relate to the areas of your study and interest. Joining groups provides you with a one-connection link to all other members within that group. These one-connection links will let you view their profiles and request introductions and will help build your network. Don't just join the group, join the conversation.

If you can contribute to the threads, jump in to provide your insights but be genuine and accurate. If you don't know anything about the topic, just stay out of it. Don't spam groups by asking for jobs or connections either, as it will not be tolerated by the administrators and you will be banned.

LinkedIn allows you to post updates to your profile, which are similar to how your Facebook updates work. Each update will show up on all of your connections' update feeds and some will appear in the e-mails that LinkedIn periodically sends.

Before a job interview, ask for the names of those who will be conducting the interview. Look them up in LinkedIn to determine their roles, background, and interests. This information will allow you to ask more relevant questions during the interview. Do not connect with these people until after the interview. Keep in mind that if they are active LinkedIn users, they will be able to see that you viewed their profile. That is fine because it shows that you are doing research before the interview process.

After your interview, you should make a connection with those who interviewed you. Make sure you connect within a day or two of the interview so that they see you have ambition to follow through and are genuinely interested in their job posting and company. Take this opportunity to thank them for the interview when making the connection.

Keep in mind that if they do accept your connection request, all of your connections will see that you two are now connected on LinkedIn. This could be a major problem if you are making connections with people outside of the normal circumstances, which may tip your hand that you are interviewing with them. Consider these consequences when making a connection on LinkedIn, or disable the option to show updates to your profile temporarily.

Once you do land your perfect job, make sure that you update your profile as soon as reasonably possible. Do not update it before you receive a signed employee agreement. All job changes that you make are included in periodic updates that LinkedIn will display to all of your connections, and you don't want to update your employment changes prematurely. You may want to wait until after your first day of employment before changing your job status. No one wants to get congratulations on a job that falls through at the last minute.

Leverage LinkedIn to connect with people you want to build a relationship with by asking your connections to make an introduction. If you have a second- or third-level connection to someone from whom you would like to request a job interview or mentorship, use LinkedIn to have one of your connections make an introduction for you. Be genuine with your request and don't just request a connection; make the most of every opportunity by asking for a specific request, like coffee or a phone call.

Of all the social media platforms, LinkedIn is the one that will have the most impact on your job search. Mastering LinkedIn is well worth the effort.

LinkedIn Guidelines

- Keep everything on your LinkedIn profile professional and genuine. Be yourself, authentic, and human.
- List all your college history, along with clubs and groups you were affiliated with during your college days.
- Add executive roles you held in clubs or groups to show your management skills.
- Don't list career-unrelated jobs. If you worked as a short-order cook throughout college, you can probably skip that employment history.
- Expand on college projects, especially if they are career related.
- All avatars should be professional and consistent across all social media platforms.

- Make sure your profile is as close to 100% complete as possible. LinkedIn has a wizard to walk you through each section.
- Try to post weekly status updates about trade-specific news or announcements to keep your profile familiar with your connections.
- All employers want employees who can communicate well, so make sure your profile has been proofread and edited by someone other than you.

Twitter

Twitter is a very easy platform to use effectively in building your personal brand. It is not required to have a Twitter profile to build a brand, but it is one of the platforms that you should consider leveraging. With its 140-character tweet limits, you are forced to downsize your communication to small chunks of insight or knowledge, ideally for pushing links to content.

Twitter is used to promote both personal and professional messages within the same platform, so there is no need to keep it only professional. If you choose to include Twitter in your social media plan, let it be the platform that makes you human by posting your personal interests and insights alongside professional content. Just keep it all clean.

All information on Twitter is completely open to the public, in general. Unless you make your profile private to only people you follow, anyone can read your profile and your tweets, review your followers and see who is following you, and view any tweets that reference you. Keep this in mind because you will not know who is reading your tweets or viewing your profile. Never tweet anything that could be considered offensive to a prospective employer. In general, don't tweet negative posts, and keep everything positive and informational.

One way to leverage Twitter in your job search is to focus on tweeting links and stories that are related to your career goals and build yourself as an authority on one topic. Combine this topic with your own insight, but also retweet and interact with those who are already topic authorities on Twitter. Follow your favorite blogs and news sites for new and relevant content which you can push through your Twitter stream to help build that authority.

Don't worry about your Twitter follower count, but instead focus on your content. Even if you only have a few followers, keep tweeting and engaging with those in your areas of interest. On Twitter, no one cares who you follow, so follow as many or as few people as you want. Feel free to follow your favorite actors and businesses, and feel free to interact with your Twitter community.

Make sure that you tweet your own content as well; don't be someone who only pushes other people's content. Use your blog as a way to create your own content. Each blog post should be tweeted multiple times throughout the week it is posted, and even following up a week or two later is valuable.

Twitter can be very time consuming, so make sure you don't get sucked into reading thousands of tweets per day (or per hour). Limit yourself to fifteen to twenty minutes per day and spend more time on your blog and LinkedIn, where you will see a direct benefit during your job search.

Applications like BufferApp and Hootsuite make it easy to schedule tweets and monitor narrow topics of interest to save yourself from getting sucked into wasting time on Twitter. Remember, your goal is to get a job, not to build a Twitter following.

Twitter Guidelines

- Be yourself, be authentic, and be human on Twitter. This is the one platform on which you should share personal interests and insight, even if it is not relevant to your industry.

- Avoid excessive tweeting about nonsense topics, as an employer may see this as something that will be an issue during work hours. If you are sending hundreds of tweets per day, you should consider cutting back.
- Try to tweet at least once or twice per day about your areas in your profession.
- As you are working on projects, feel free to tweet your challenges and successes as short updates. This shows that you are human and are actually working.
- Twitter is the perfect platform to catch up on industry news. Follow those in your industry who are great at curating content and engage or retweet their posts.

Facebook

Facebook is the number-one platform where job seekers can ruin their chance of getting an interview, and this is especially true with recent graduates. Many people think that Facebook is a private network and only your friends can view your posts, pictures, and friends, but that is not entirely true. In general, friends of friends can see your posts, and there is a good chance the person that you are interviewing with has at least one friend in common with you. It is best to take the high road with Facebook.

Facebook is quickly losing popularity with high school and college students as they migrate to other platforms like Twitter, Instagram, and Snapchat. So if you are one of those who migrated from Facebook, keep in mind that your account probably still exists and may be extremely out of date.

You do not need to delete your Facebook account; you just need to be aware of what others may see and how to represent yourself in the best way possible. You may be tempted to use Facebook to promote yourself to future employers. However, you should actually use

Facebook as a personal social media platform only, a place where you can communicate with your friends and family, not your boss or future boss. Generally speaking, do not let your Facebook overlap with your professional network.

I already covered how to clean up your Facebook profile in an earlier chapter, but if you skipped that, pause reading and go back to do it now. Plenty of prospective employees have been eliminated from consideration based solely on what they had posted to Facebook, so don't let that happen to you.

If a prospective employer reaches out to you through Facebook, it would be advisable to *not* accept their friend request. They may be trying to get closer to your Facebook posts, friends, or photos. Instead of accepting the friend request, politely reply that you keep your Facebook private, and push them over to your LinkedIn or Twitter accounts instead.

It is fine to post on Facebook that you are looking for a job (as long as any current boss you have already knows that you are looking for a new job) and even the successes that you have had through the journey, but keep it clean and professional. It is best to not name companies that you are interviewing with, because you never know who might have a story to tell about you.

Facebook Guidelines

- Keep your Facebook profile private for your friends and family.
- Always be cautious about what you post to Facebook, since friends of a friend will be able to see your posts.
- Never post content on Facebook that you would not feel comfortable talking about with coworkers at the office.
- Frequently check to see how the world sees your Facebook profile by logging out and then looking at your profile page. That is what *anyone* can see of your profile.

- Make sure no one tags you in inappropriate photos. It would be wise to disable the option for anyone to automatically tag you without your permission.
- Never post anything about where you are interviewing on your Facebook wall.

YouTube and Other Video Platforms

Video is such a great medium for teaching knowledge and sharing skills with others, but YouTube is not for everyone. If you are unable to professionally represent yourself with good audio and video editing, it would be best to skip this platform entirely. Luckily, the cost of producing high-quality video has never been cheaper, as most cell phones can shoot in high-definition.

With very little training required and free software available, anyone who wants to become competent enough to use video can do so quickly. Video is the next frontier of social media and putting in the time now, while there are fewer competitors, can definitely set you apart from the pack.

One great way to set yourself apart from the other candidates would be to produce a series of training videos for an open source project. Pick a project that you are participating in on GitHub and turn a written tutorial into a video series. Upload the videos to YouTube, or another platform like Vimeo, and then link the video back to your personal website, write a blog post with it, and promote your video directly on the GitHub page.

Employers are always looking for employees who can take the initiative to see a need, solve the problem, and promote their solution. Being a good educator and trainer is a great skill that will spark an employer's interest in hiring you.

Consider integrating video into a few blog posts as well, making them a video-blog post. There are many screen-recording programs like Join.me, which are very easy to use and can capture your screen along with your audio. A short video of a product review or framework integration can really enhance a blog post. Make sure it looks and sounds professional. The optimal viewing length is less than two minutes, so you should edit it down to just the best content.

Video has quickly become a medium to learn and leverage in marketing and branding.

YouTube Guidelines

- Promote your YouTube channel yourself by adding links to your videos on other channels.
- Keep your videos professional with good editing and quality audio, and draft a rough script so you can remember your content.
- Since video cannot be searched, always include a thorough description and transcript if possible in the post.

Pinterest and Tumblr

Tumblr and Pinterest are excellent platforms to build your personal brand and portfolio if you are pursuing a career that will leverage your design skills. As a companion to their blog, artists and designers can push their artwork to these platforms while building their portfolio.

Pinterest would be an excellent way for a designer to engage and build boards by pinning their ideas, designs, and styles. Selecting the complementary colors, styles, and fonts is an art form. If you have an eye for design, Pinterest has a great way for you to demonstrate those skills to prospective employers.

Mixing both professional thoughts with your personal interests is also a great way to build your Pinterest portfolio. Pin items that you find visually appealing that you may work into future projects as well, because having a good base of ideas is a huge plus for prospective employers. Promote and discuss your desire for finding art and design during your interviews. Make sure your Pinterest boards reflect your brand.

Tumblr is a platform where you can upload your own photos, videos, or art to interact with others using a microblog format. Push as much of your work as you can into Tumblr and leverage Pinterest to organize those into the appropriated boards and series.

Tumblr and Pinterest Guidelines

- Only leverage these platforms if you they are part of your overall career plan.
- Cross-populate your posts through LinkedIn, Twitter, and Facebook where applicable to hit the largest audiences.

Other Social Media

Many industries have subsocial media platforms like Wattpad for authors and GitHub for developers. Any platform that is relevant to your future career is relevant to your portfolio. Follow the same guidelines as you would with other social media platforms. Keep them professional with a personal feel, and post or update each platform frequently.

Remember to keep your personal branding consistent. Use the same avatar across all platforms so prospective employers do not need to guess if this is your work or someone's with a similar name. It is best to also use the same username or handle on each platform. You should avoid cute names or nicknames that you may not want to follow you for the rest of your business career. Using your name or a slight variation of your name is often best.

Write a consistent description of yourself that you use on each platform as part of your bio. For many platforms, you can use your bio that you write in the chapter on developing your brand.

Before focusing on new platforms, make sure your profiles are dominating on the key social media platforms. Learn to use one or two consistently and well before expanding.

V. SUMMARY

Networking is the best way to get your name out there as a potential job candidate. Attend as many networking and social groups within your community as possible during your job search. Networking does more than just increase your network; it helps prepare you for social engagements like interviewing. The more comfortable you are with socializing and talking about yourself, the better you will do in job interviews.

Not everyone is born with an innate ability to socialize and network, but like everything else in life, the only way to get better is to practice. While networking, you will get asked what you do over and over again, which will allow you practice and refine the skill of talking about yourself, your skills, and your portfolio. Notice how people resonate with how you describe yourself and the follow-up questions that they have. Adjust your personal pitch to account for areas that people positively or negatively respond to when you network to zero in on your ideal personal description. Networking events are great ways to practice interview skills with multiple people in a few hours, allowing you to quickly adjust your pitch.

These events are also a great place to meet business leaders and get your name known in the community as an authority on a topic and someone who is in search of a new career. Don't hesitate to talk about your goals, dream career, or work portfolio, because you never know who you are talking to at a social event; it may be your next boss.

Many communities have social events that allow anyone to present a short presentation. This is another way to build your personal brand of authority on a topic. Volunteer to present on a topic that you are familiar with; it will build your brand as well as provide you valuable practice with public speaking on the topic. The more comfortable you are talking in front of a group, the better you will do with a one-on-one job interview. Consider presenting on one of your work portfolio projects.

Above all, always be promoting yourself at every event you attend. Hand out your business cards with your website and contact information to everyone you meet. Suggest that they review your portfolio work and pass on your contact information to those who are hiring for your skills. Handing out business cards will help people remember later that they met you and gives you an opportunity to get their business card as well. Remember to be respectful, be considerate, ask questions about others, and avoid dominating the conversation. As soon as possible, look up those you spoke with on LinkedIn and send them a connection request to build your social network.

In general, you should not hand out your résumé at a networking event. You should have a number of copies ready if someone asks for one, but do not lead into a conversation by handing someone your résumé. Always be prepared for an impromptu interview, but avoid seeming desperate or inconsiderate.

Action steps for much of this advice are included in the last section of this book, in a master checklist for success.

6

BUILDING A PORTFOLIO

Every new job seeker needs a portfolio, especially if they are pursuing a technical career such as a developer. With little to no experience, the only way you can show a prospective employer your skills and knowledge is through a well-defined portfolio. I previously covered the preparation work necessary before you begin looking for a career. In this chapter, I am going to cover how to demonstrate that portfolio through a personally branded website specifically designed for your career goals.

Depending on your career goals, your portfolio will contain different information, but the core goal remains the same—demonstrating your skills to a future employer. They may see your portfolio before they call you for an interview or else after your interview. Either way, a portfolio should put your best image forward and detail your exact career goals, development skills, and knowledge.

As a developer, your portfolio should start with three key things: who you are, work you have done, and your value proposition to a business.

Who You Are

Most people have a hard time talking about themselves. The easiest way to do this is to reflect on your life and pick out the highlights you are proudest of, even if they are not important to your career. Remember, employers are hiring people not skills, so you need to be personable.

This element can be in the form of a brief summary of who you are, what you enjoy doing, and achievements that make you proud. For example, if you have won a state spelling bee, mention how it made you feel when you won and what words put you over the top. A few paragraphs is all it takes. You want to demonstrate that you are personable.

Another great way to demonstrate who you are is to volunteer at an organization whose missions you feel passionate about. For example, if you love animals, maybe you can volunteer there to help promote an upcoming pet food drive.

Work You Have Done

All portfolios need to demonstrate your work experiences with actual examples. Since you might not have a lot of real-world work experience, here is your opportunity to demonstrate your skills.

Examples of websites that you have built are really easy; just point them to your work. If your experience is offline or not something that can be viewed publicly, do your best to explain what you have done and the challenges you overcame while working on the project.

This content is the perfect way to demonstrate your value to an organization.

Your Value Proposition

A value proposition is your promise of value that will be delivered. We all have them. Some of us take this value more seriously than others. Your résumé should show what your value proposition is to your potential new employer. This is easily said but not always easily done in a résumé.

You want to avoid the cliché buzz words like hard worker, good listener, and so on—you know what they are. Instead, put your work portfolio in the context of what the business would expect from you as an employee. Instead of saying you are hard worker, show it by explaining the specifics of a portfolio project about the number of hours and that you learned a specific skill set while doing so and this is how you attack every problem.

For example, your value proposition might be something like:

- My experience building mobile applications saves your business money on training.
- My minor in marketing will allow you to offer a new service to clients.
- The network I have built with my freelance work will be great new clients for your organization.
- My passion for great customer support will make me the ideal candidate to lead large projects with difficult customers.

Now that we've addressed the first three things to cover in your portfolio, let's discuss enriching your portfolio in three steps:

1. Building a personally branded website to act as your digital résumé.
2. Showing real-world experience through projects.
3. Constructing a social media campaign to showcase your skills, goals, and experience.

I. BUILDING A PERSONALLY BRANDED WEBSITE

Think of your personally branded website as your new résumé. Some companies would rather see your website than a résumé anyway. If you are one of five candidates and you are the only one who can demonstrate your skills instead of explaining your skills, you will have a huge advantage over the others. However, many companies will still require a paper résumé as part of their policy, even if it is not actually reviewed by those who are doing the hiring. Everything that would be in a well-constructed résumé should be on your personal website, and more. After all, a résumé is flat and one-dimensional, which is very boring. Your website shouldn't be.

In all cases, you must have a personal website that is your home base for employers to review your experience and portfolio. I have even heard from some employers who ask candidates to send them their LinkedIn profiles instead of their résumés. These platforms are easy to use, won't cost you a dime, and will reinforce your personal brand. Your personal website is just that: personal. Show your work, but also show what you are passionate about, especially with non-work-related passions, within reason. If you're a prolific party animal, you might want to find other hobbies to talk about.

Treat your personal website as a business that advertises you as an asset, someone with freelance skills. You may never do a paid freelance project, but representing yourself as a freelancer demonstrates your ambition and self-motivation. Occasionally employers may want to hire you for a trial period before committing to a job offer. If you represent yourself as a freelancer, you may get that opportunity to be paid to demonstrate your skills and land a job. In fact, most companies will hire a freelancer first before they commit to a full-time employee. This gives you an "in" with the company as a freelancer.

Before I tackle design, let's cover functionality: what your personal website will contain. A personalized website will contain the following sections, features, and content:

- Main page – to quickly show your portfolio.
- Portfolio – a portfolio section that contains links to, descriptions of, and examples of your portfolio work.

- Social links – a section with links to your social media profiles.
- Blog – a personal blog that demonstrates your ability to communicate through the written word.
- And finally, an "About" page where you will talk all about you and your background.

That's it. Not twenty links in the navigation bar, just those five. Now, let's get started with a design and then get your site up and running.

Design

Website design is critical in setting the tone of your personal brand. The design of your site, from templates to widgets all the way down to photos and colors, is a direct reflection of your personal brand and how people will see you as a prospective employee. Keep this in mind when choosing your design.

Depending on your career goals, you will choose one of these two design paths:

- If you are pursuing a software developer career where you plan on writing back-end code instead of front-end code, pick a professional template and don't mess with it. Your career choice is not about design, but rather development, so spend your time building a portfolio around code instead of user interface. Pick a good theme and move on.
- If you are pursuing a user-interface design career, pick a basic template and spend some time modifying it to meet your specific brand and style. This helps reinforce your skills by building a beautiful design from the raw template. You need a unique design and implementation, so focus your portfolio work around those design and implementation skills.

Before I dive into the specifics of website design, let's review the purpose of design. Regardless of career, your website should operate like any other website and aim to hold the reader's attention. You may not be selling books or reviewing movies, but you are providing everything a future employer needs to know about you. If they bounce off the site after thirty seconds, you failed your design challenge and possibly your interview chances.

Make sure your design allows for a personal blog. It may sound odd to write a blog if you're pursuing a software developer career, but keep in mind we are setting you apart from the pack. If you can demonstrate that you have the ability to communicate through writing, you quickly become a more valuable prospective employee. Do not dread this type of writing; it is less work than you think.

The best way to determine a good design and style for your personal website is spending a few hours reviewing other successful personal websites. Instead of creating a design from scratch, use work from others and tweak it to make it personal. I am not advocating copying someone else's site outright, but leverage what others have already figured out for your benefit.

Start by looking at personal websites of others in your career field. A great way to find relevant personal websites is by identifying those in similar careers via LinkedIn or Twitter. After all, you want their jobs, so why not start emulating how they represent themselves to the community? Take the ideas you like best from each site and build custom variations of those themes. The next two sections personalize these skills for software developers, system admins, and design-oriented developers.

Now Go Execute

- Pick a WordPress hosting company. There are hundreds of them out there (I like Flywheel [http://getflywheel.com] for $15/month), but other free options are available. Unless you absolutely cannot afford $100 per year, I strongly suggest you use a paid service. You get what you pay for, and a free service may be slow or unexpectedly be offline. The last thing you want is for a prospective employer to get an error when going to your website.

- Create a website. I recommend using WordPress; it is the most common platform with many templates and plugins. But if you want to use another CMS platform, go right ahead and use a simple static website: Drupal, Concrete 5, etc.

- Ideally, you'll build your own theme through a custom theme that matches your personal brand. It is fine to start with an existing theme that gets you close, but make sure you build enough to justify your developer title.

- Register a custom domain name to map to your personal website; this costs between $10–$20 per year, but adds professionalism to your site. Make sure you pick a professional domain as well, since you are being judged at every level.

- Move on to the next element. Do not spend days on this step—pick a good template and move on, since it is easy to switch later.

II. DEMONSTRATING YOUR PORTFOLIO

Your portfolio (your personal website) can be published with different styles and templates. Pick one which reflects your personal brand. Your website's main page will cover all the important details about you, your work portfolio, and your personal brand. Think of this page as your thirty-second elevator pitch showcasing your best work for everyone to see.

Hosted WordPress platforms provide you with a vanity domain name to use and will typically be something like *[account].hostedsite. com*. This is fine to get your website up and running, but I recommend you buy a personal domain name to map to your website. There are many very inexpensive top-level-domains you can register for as little as $10 per year. Businesses should operate under the ".com" top-level-domain whenever possible because consumers will expect a .com. A personal website can easily operate under a ".me" or a ".info" domain, whichever is easiest to build around your brand.

Your personal website should have the following pages, each dedicated to their unique function for your portfolio and personal brand:

About Me: Outlines for a prospective employer who you are. This is where you want to be as personal as possible—remember to be your authentic self. Information that can be listed includes your hobbies, where you grew up, networking groups that you belong to, favorite websites, organizations you support, and a brief summary about you. Make sure nothing could be considered offensive to anyone viewing your website, even if it is your passion. For example, if you are an avid hunter, it is fine to list your passions but do not post pictures of animals you have killed, as that may offend a prospective employer. Never give an employer a reason to reject you from consideration.

Social Media: It is beneficial for you to promote exactly where employers can find you on social media platforms. After all, they will find you eventually, so let's make it easy with a thorough list of links. Having a list of all of your accounts in one spot allows you to also control exactly how they find you on each platform. If you are not the only person in the world with your name, this also eliminates them finding the wrong profile and possibly rejecting you by mistake. List all profiles you actively use; I cover how to use social media in the "Social Media" chapter.

Résumé: Even though your website contains more information than will fit on a traditional one-page paper résumé, you still need a résumé. I will cover résumé content in the "Résumé" chapter, but your website should have a dedicated page for your résumé. Your résumé page should have all the standard résumé information plus a link to download a printable version which must be in PDF format.

Portfolio and Experience: Even though much of the information that comprises your portfolio will be spread around your website and personal blog, you will want one page with a short summary and links to your work. In some cases, these will be links to your GitHub and Upwork profile and open-source projects in which you participate. Include links to websites you have built to demonstrate your experience.

Blog: Prominently display your blog content for everyone to see, whether it is on the same website or a separate blogging site. Promote your most recent blog post on the landing page so you can show the blog is active. WordPress has a built-in blog platform that's easy to incorporate within your personal website. I recommend using WordPress for both your website and blog. Don't blog unless you are willing to commit to doing it at least once a week; more about that later.

Newsletter Form: It is not required to have a newsletter, but consider adding one anyway. You may never send a single newsletter e-mail, but having one will bring additional legitimacy to your website. Platforms such as MailChimp and ConstantContact make it easy to build a contact list and send e-mails. These platforms cost you nothing at the basic levels except the time to set them up.

Contact: Lastly, do not forget to advertise exactly how people can contact you. The last thing you want is a prospective employer trying to make an outreach but being unable to find an easy way to contact you. It is unwise to list your e-mail address as text since it can be scraped by spammers, or your phone number since that may mean you receive unwanted telemarketing calls. Each web platform will have a contact form you can use that sends a message into your e-mail account, and that is the best method for using on your website.

Remember, the sooner you set up your personal website, the more time you have to refine the content. Don't rush to get everything done in a few hours, because it will look thrown-together and devalue your brand.

Now Go Execute

- Set up a website through a hosted platform; WordPress is recommended.
- Create a new page for each of the items outlined above.
- Create a menu for the four items—portfolio, social media links, blog, and About page.
- Write content for each page. List your top portfolio items and experience on the main page as well.
- Setup an e-mail newsletter platform if you want, and add the plugin to your WordPress website so it appears as a widget.
- Create a widget that appears on every page containing your contact form link, your résumé link, and a brief personal summary. This identifies your website as a personal brand website.

III. INTEGRATING SOCIAL MEDIA

Your personal website should have links to all your social media profiles where you actively post content or participate in the community. Employers will track you down on social media, often before they ever call you for an interview. Use this to your advantage by making it easy for prospective employers to get to know you. There are three reasons you want to promote your social profiles and content: 1) it gives you an opportunity for them to get to know you; 2) it shows that you are an authority who understands technology; and 3) it demonstrates that you know how to communicate.

The reason you want a dedicated web page for your social media icons is to allow you to control and inform a prospective employer about who you are. For example, if you have a YouTube channel that you use to stream your favorite video game hacks to your friends, don't hide that but rather put it in the right context. Provide a description for this link as something that you are passionate about and love to share with your friends, even though it is not relevant to your current professional life. Employers will appreciate your honesty and the fact that you are socially balanced with hobbies (and friends) outside of work. Above everything else, you must be authentic and genuine with your content.

On the other hand, if you rant about local businesses by posting disturbing photos of restaurant bathrooms on your Tumblr site, make sure that does not make it back to your personal website or your brand. Consider deleting that account outright or rebrand it under a pseudonym with a completely different name and avatar. Make sure when you search for yourself online that this page does not show up. You should completely separate yourself from this type of negative social media during your job search.

Now that we have a web page to link to your social media accounts, let's cover how your website, blog, and social media content will interact with each other.

There are many WordPress plugins that allow you to integrate your social media activity (a list of your latest posts) into your personal website, but do not use them unless your content is one hundred percent professional. That's the wrong approach to the integration your content. Think about someone who might be reviewing your website and see a stream of tweets that you just made about dinner—those do not belong on your website! Social media and website content are consumed differently, so treat them accordingly.

Highly creative fields can be more relaxed about integrating personal and professional content, but in the software engineering field, it's best not to integrate social media feeds directly into your website.

Your social media content should stay on the respective social media platforms. The reverse is not necessarily true. Your blog content should be published to all of your social media channels, often published repeatedly over time. There are many WordPress plugins that will automatically post your new blog content to all of your social media channels. This works very well to drive communication back to your blog since people are more likely to share a tweet than they are to share a blog post.

Posting your blog content to your social media channels will also help build your credibility as someone who knows how to write and distribute content.

Lastly, do not promote inactive social media accounts. If you have a Google+ account only because you have a Gmail account, do not include Google+ on your social media page. Also, do not create a social media presence with the sole intent of showing that you have a presence on that platform. No one is going to care if you only use one or two social media platforms, as long as you use them appropriately.

Now Go Execute

- Create a web page on your personal website with a short description and link to each of your social media profiles.
- Ensure each social media platform is up to date with avatars and professional content.
- Set up a WordPress plugin to auto-post new blog posts to select social media accounts.
- Review how each social media platform conveys your personal brand.

IV. PERSONAL BLOGGING

In addition to having a personal website as a résumé, each job seeker should also have a blog. Many may feel that blogging has been replaced by social media, and they are correct that it has, but it is still a very valuable tool for job seekers. Your blog will probably never be as popular as your Twitter account, Facebook wall, or Tumblr page, but it is an important way to demonstrate your professionalism in your chosen career field and your ability to communicate with more than 140 characters. Social media is a poor way for employers to judge your communication skills, while a blog is the ideal format.

You should commit to writing a blog as part of your career plans. It may sound like a daunting task if you have never done it before, but once you break it down, it is actually a very reasonable and a doable goal. Plus, it will set you apart from the other candidates and you want to differentiate yourself at every opportunity possible. Commit to posting one blog post per week and have at least six months' worth of blog posts online before your first interview. That may seem like a huge commitment, but it's only about twenty-five posts, and it is fine to skip a few weeks so let's call it twenty posts.

There is no reason to write the equivalent of a novella or novel for each blog post, and in fact your posts should be short on purpose, as short as two hundred to three hundred words works best (about three paragraphs!). Keeping your posts short also demonstrates your ability to get to a point quickly while still being able to communicate with your peers. If you love to write, go right ahead write and 1,200-word epic blog posts, but that length is definitely not required. And keep in mind, those 1,200-word epic posts will likely get skimmed anyway.

Another tactic you can use is to break a long blog post into a multi-part series. This allows you to keep talking about the same topic across multiple weeks and offer a final conclusion post. It is easier to promote a multipost series rather than one-off posts as well. Just make sure each one can stand alone too.

WordPress will allow you to pre-date blog posts, so if you did not start your blog six months ago, you are still fine. Create a bunch of blog posts, predate them evenly throughout the past six months, and you've got yourself a "long standing" blog as part of your portfolio. Remember to be authentic, and do not just post fluff content!

Each blog post should follow a similar style and format and stay true to your brand. Keeping each of them consistent with the same flow will ensure authenticity. Pick a simple outline for your style, make a note of it somewhere, and then follow it for each post. You can draft off this flow to help get you started:

- What are you going to write about?
- Why is this interesting?
- How has this helped you/others in accomplishing a task/goal/ project?
- What should your reader do now?

Using an outline will help you form your thoughts more quickly and stay on topic. This will build a rhythm across your entire blog. Remember, you are not trying to win any blogging awards (yes, they do exist); you only want to demonstrate your ability to communicate and start to establish yourself as an authority in your chosen field. It would be ideal if all of your blog posts were on a single theme, but if you feel more scattered and want to cover many themes, that is fine as well.

Choose blog topics that are relevant to you or your career path. If you are pursuing a career as a developer, talk about the latest development tools, review a new version of a framework, or demonstrate how you implemented something. Since you'll already be working on building a portfolio of work projects, you obviously have a few active projects under development—talk about them and your successes or failures.

It is fine to throw in a few off-topic blog posts as well, but make sure you tie them back to you or your career field with a conclusion sentence. If Formula One racing is your thing, write a post comparing the latest engine types and how technology has played a role in that rapidly changing sport. Above all, everything you write about needs to reflect your personal brand.

Keep a notepad—either physical or digital—and jot down future topic ideas. This will be helpful when you later sit down to hammer out four or five new posts at a time. Turn to social media or tech blogs for ideas as well.

These are some topics that you should avoid writing about:

- Your job hunt and the interviews that you have conducted—never talk about these!
- Any negative reviews of anything. Resist the urge to blog about negative topics entirely.
- Deeply personal stories. Save those for Facebook-only posts among friends and family.
- Avoid anything that could be considered controversial by a prospective employer. You may think everyone agrees with your beliefs, but that won't be the case.
- Social events that could be viewed as immature or irresponsible. You know what we're referring to!

Writing a two-hundred- to three-hundred-word blog post should take you about fifteen to twenty minutes, tops. If you find yourself leaving posts to the last minute each week and are constantly missing your weekly post goals, write five or six at a time when you have an hour. You will find that it is faster to write multiple posts at once anyway. Take longer posts and split them up into multiple posts when appropriate with a separate conclusion post.

Since this is part of your career portfolio, make absolutely sure that each post represents you and demonstrates your views, style, and skills in a positive light. Check for spelling errors, grammatical errors, and that the blog post actually flows. If possible, find a blogging companion so you can proof and edit each other's posts. It is always best to have a second (or third) set of eyes on each post before publishing. Share your personal branding worksheet with your editor so that they can help you reinforce your brand with each post.

It is much easier to blog with a written schedule and a plan instead of just when you think about it. Otherwise, you may find that blog posts get made hastily and this will show you as being sloppy and not professional.

Still unsure what to write about? Try Googling phrases related to new development trends or top-ten technology lists.

Writing niche content about topics you are passionate about hones your skills and will even help you truly identify your passions in the technology field.

Now Go Execute

- The simplest way to get started is to jump right in. Set a timer for sixty minutes, close your web browser, and write four or five blog posts. Don't worry about spelling or grammar errors during the first draft—just write. Every fifteen minutes, start a new post. Once you are done, set it aside for a few hours or a day and then come back to edit them.
- Find a partner to proofread and review your blog posts. A professional editor may charge about $20–$25 per 2,000 words. Check out Upwork.com for a list of freelance editors.
- Write and predate twenty blog posts when you first start your blog site.
- Schedule eight blog posts to run over the next two months and put this task on the back burner for a while.
- Keep your brand in mind for every post that you write. Ask yourself if each post matches how you want the world to view you and your skills. If not, revise.

V. FINAL TOUCHES

By now you will have a pretty rich personal website framework that demonstrates who you are, your skills, and your experiences. You may not have content for every page yet, but it should start to look pretty good. I am going to cover a few final touches that will help tie your website together.

You need a great-looking avatar image. Don't use a thumbnail of your favorite actor or actress, a game character, or some weird piece of art that only means something to you. It should be a small, clean, easy to identify head shot of you! (Imagine that: your picture of you should be you.) And make sure that the same avatar is used on every platform—this helps reinforce that the profile is actually yours. Avatars help to provide the glue that ties all of your profiles together. Don't make an employer guess if they have your correct profile.

A professional photographer may charge an expensive fee, but paying for professional headshots may not be necessary, although they will look awesome. A simple cell phone camera is capable of taking a good enough photo for this purpose. If the quality is not what you want, you can always convert the photo to gray scale, which will hide a lot of the imperfections without losing the essence of having an accurate photo so people know it is you. Just make sure that the background is appropriate and not distracting.

During your job search, make sure you keep your blog content fresh. If you absolutely hate writing a weekly blog post, don't sweat it. Just hunker down and write six over the weekend and then schedule them to be posted once a week for the next six weeks. Done. Now you can focus on building your portfolio, writing code, and building your network.

Remember that this is a personal website, so make sure you bring in that personable feel as well. Don't make it so dry that your reader thinks you are a robot or an autogenerated website. If you are passionate about a project, explain why you feel that way. It does not need to be deeply personal. After all, you are a human, so be genuine with everything you post.

And finally, but probably the most important task, have everything reviewed and edited by someone else. Make absolutely sure that your content is as clean and refined as possible. If a prospective employer is reviewing your website and finds repeated spelling errors, they are likely to mark it against you as a potential candidate. Don't let this happen on something so trivial as editing.

Now Go Execute

- Update your social media avatars with a professional-looking headshot.
- Be human and stay genuine with your personal website, blog content, and experiences.
- Proof, polish, and edit your personal website, blog, and résumé.

7

PREPARING FOR THE INTERVIEW

Over the years, I have interviewed a lot of potential employees, and most of them have been ill-prepared for the interview. This is your chance to set yourself apart from all other candidates. Confidence will go a long way during an interview, and confidence is gained by preparation.

The number-one mistake I see from first-time interviewees is showing up late. And it is such an easy mistake to overcome. One time I had a college student who showed up about twenty minutes late for an interview. It was clear that he was completely frazzled when he sat down and there was no way he was going to be able to conduct a professional interview. He tried to plan ahead by having a friend drive him the forty minutes to our office, but they ended up getting stuck in the ditch after hitting a patch of ice. No one was hurt and they were able to get themselves out, but that incident just threw him off and it was clear that no matter how good of a candidate he was, he had lost all confidence that morning.

Another time I had a candidate show up just a few minutes late, but since she was late she started to panic and ran up the flight of stairs to our office. This left her out of breath when she came through our door and she simply couldn't recover from the anxiety during the thirty-minute interview.

1. YOUR RÉSUMÉ

There is a steady shift away from the traditional one-page résumé toward an online digital portfolio. There are two digital options that work well for technical professionals—your personal website and your LinkedIn profile page. This shift is a huge win for technical professions because résumés are just too flat to tell your full story. If you do everything described in this book, your résumé will be your portfolio website. Some businesses will accept your website, or even your LinkedIn profile, as your résumé, but many large companies will still insist that you submit a traditional résumé along with a cover letter and references, mostly to meet outdated policies. Luckily, now that you have everything ready on your website, it will be quick for you to pull together a traditional résumé.

Your résumé needs to look professional by focusing on your skills and experience over your actual work history. Employers do not want to see unrelated jobs or fluffed up buzzwords like "hard working" or "self-motivated." A good résumé will have three primary sections: your skills, your experience, and your education. Let's cover these three sections specifically:

Your Skills: Focus on relevant skills, skills that your future employer will actually care about. Do not list things like "reliable" or "hard worker," because you probably would not have gotten this far in life if you were unreliable and lazy. Instead, list the skills that you have learned through building your portfolio and make sure you put them in the right context. Good skills are action words along with a trait, like "efficient in optimizing SQL queries" or "developed multiple iPhone applications." Keep skills to a multicolumn bullet list. Something that is an overall highlight of what you know about the industry will work best for employers.

Your Experience: Experience is what makes you valuable to an employer and it will demonstrate your ability to contribute as a team member. For each of your major work experiences, give the job a title and write a few sentences about your experience. Focus on your successes, not your tasks. An example might be:

"Published 'Happy Task,' an iPhone Application—developed an efficient task management application that auto-syncs with your calendar and Evernote, eliminating multiple task lists on your phone. Happy Task has a five-star rating with an audience base of about five hundred active users achieved in the first three months after release."

List the top three or four experiences that you want a future employer to focus on while considering your application. If there are others, list them in a quick list and point viewers to your website for a more detailed list of each project. You never know what an employer may see as a relevant experience or skill set they are looking for in a new candidate.

Your Education: Lastly, list your education with the newest degree or certificate at the top. If you have great gaps in your education that are not easily explainable, simply eliminate the exact dates of your education. List all education you have, even the degrees or certifications that may not be directly relevant to the career you are pursuing today.

Remember that education is not just a traditional college degree either. If you have earned specific certifications or taken additional classes, list those along with your scores if they are relevant. This is where you will list any code boot camps that you attended, along with your Startup Weekends, Hackathons, Meetups, and similar entrepreneurial events. List any volunteer work. If you volunteer for a nonprofit where you have learned skills for operating a business, list that as a real-world educational experience, either under experience or education.

Workshops and major conferences should also be listed under education. It shows that you are more well-rounded than someone with a cookie-cutter college degree.

Lastly, do not forget to be human. Your résumé should weave in what makes you unique. Work in what makes you passionate about technology, including your non-technology hobbies and your life goals. They are not hiring you just because of your experience; they are hiring you the person, so make them feel a bond with you as a human. Many books on résumés will say that you should never list personal things on your résumé. The problem with this is that you come off as just another warm body with nothing that an employer could bond with. Use this to your advantage by connecting at a personal level with those reading your résumé. But make sure it comes off as professional at the same time. If you are passionate about video games, instead of mentioning the all-nighters, mention that you moderate the game's message board or that you host gaming parties on the weekend for friends. Give yourself every opportunity possible for your interviewer to find something that they have in common with you, because everyone likes to find commonality during a conversation.

In addition to a résumé, create business cards with all of your contact information and your website addresses. Sites like VistaPrint offer a great way to design and order business cards for as little as $20. Handing out a business card will help people remember that they met you and it gives you an opportunity to get their business card at the same time. Your business card should list your name, phone number, e-mail address, and your website. If you have a personal brand with a logo, use that as well but don't feel you need one.

Another great way to stand out from the other candidates is to print out your résumé and value proposition, put it in a nice folder or envelope, and hand deliver it to the business who is doing the hiring. Walk into the business and to the person at the front desk, say something like, "You have a job opening for [position], I wanted to hand deliver my résumé to you. Can you get this to [person doing hiring]?" Expect that they will simply take your résumé and thank you, but if you did this at my business, whoever answered the door would ask you to wait while they went to get the person you were delivering the résumé to. Now you have an opportunity to stand out, make a great first impression, and be prepared for an on-the-spot interview. You have nothing to lose.

If you don't get to talk to the person conducting the hiring, it would be wise to also submit your résumé through the channels recommended on the job posting as well. Whomever took your résumé may have misplaced it or delivered it to the wrong person.

Now Go Execute

- Draft your résumé today; it is never too early to have a résumé completed.
- Add your current skills, experience, and education. Skip those items that are not relevant to your future career.
- Create a digital version of your résumé on your website and update it periodically.
- If you are not going to graduate for a year or two, write the résumé that you want to have upon graduation and then start working to meet those expectations, but don't post that version online yet.

II. PREPARING FOR THE INTERVIEW

Everything we have been discussing has led up to the interview, which is obviously the most important part of any job search. Your portfolio, social media, and résumé are all meaningless if you botch the interview. While interviewing has not changed much over the years, high-technology jobs do require some special consideration to allow your true value and skills to come through during an interview.

Interviews can be very stressful, especially if you are an introvert and not the social type, which is common for those in development, IT, and other similar careers. Never fear, there are a ton of resources available to help. I will cover the basics here, but above everything else, the number-one thing to remember during an interview is to be authentic, genuine, honest, and yourself. It may sound redundant or like common sense, but the second that door closes, you will have a tendency to forget everything you know. I've seen it over and over, interviewees being so nervous that they forget to breathe, twitch uncontrollably, and answer every question as quickly as possible, just praying for the interview to end.

Here are some tips that will get you going in the right direction.

Don't Be Nervous. If you can't communicate with people you don't know, you won't excel throughout your career. You will need to work on your soft interview skills. The career department at your college or university will be able to help you overcome your nervousness through practice interviews. Remember, you will only grow if you do things outside of your comfort zone, so being nervous is a great place to start. Now you just need to overcome it through practice and preparation. I have had many college students do mock interviews with my team over the years, and it is helpful to have real-world interviews to practice.

Show Up on Time. This should go without needing to be said, but too often young, first-time job seekers mess this one up and show up late. Not always on purpose, but through a lack of planning. Don't show up thirty minutes early either, since you will likely have to sit awkwardly and wait your turn, possibly running into other candidates also being interviewed. Ideally, you should show up five to ten minutes before your scheduled interview time, which will give you a few minutes to mentally prepare. Sit down, relax, take a few deep breaths, and refresh the key three points you want to make. If you are unfamiliar with where the interview is being held, scout it out the day before. Have a quick conversation with whomever greets you, since it will help put you at ease. It doesn't need to be a deep conversation, ask them how long they have worked at the company, if they are from the area, and so on.

Prepare at Least One Side Project to Discuss. Make sure you have worked on at least one side project that you can thoroughly discuss during your interview. If you have followed my guidelines outlined in this book, you will have several to choose from. But if you have never done anything outside school work, you won't make it past the first interview. Mentally prepare in advance which project you want to dive into.

Set Yourself Apart From the Pack. You are probably one of five to ten potential candidates for the job you are interviewing for, or possibly more depending on the city. Think about your best skills and assets, and play those skills up at every opportunity you can. Bring it back to the real-world examples, because you need to demonstrate your passion about this career that you are applying for. If you are an active member of an organization, then talk about that, and talk about what you have done to help that organization. Do not rely on your education alone, since that is the one thing consistent across every other candidate being interviewed. If you can't set yourself apart from the others, you will not be victorious.

Think About How You Can Demonstrate Ambition and Passion. Play your passions to your advantage—talk about things that you are passionate about, even if they are not directly work related. When you talk about things that excite you, your enthusiasm will come through. For example, maybe you are really passionate about Formula One racing. Did you write a blog post on the topic? Make sure you spend a few minutes showing how you are passionate about life.

There is no shortage of online resources or books written about proper interview techniques. While none are dedicated to software developers, system administrators, or designers, many of the same principles will apply. Check out a few from your local library, ask your career department at your university for recommendations, or search for ones positively reviewed on online retailers.

III. PRACTICING YOUR INTERVIEW

Everyone needs to practice interviewing. With practice you will become more comfortable talking about yourself, your skills, and the authority and knowledge you bring to a prospective employer. Take this advice seriously and conduct practice interviews.

All colleges and universities have career centers that will have interview resources available to you. They will work with you on interview skills and will practice mock interviews with you. Their feedback will be invaluable, so take their advice and improve your interviewing skills, then repeat the mock interviews. Rarely does anyone land a job without an interview, so make yours the best possible.

Most career centers will host job fairs where you can interview with many companies in one day. Even if you would never work for any of the companies, take this opportunity to practice your interview skills. Aim to get ten to fifteen interviews under your belt before that dream job interview. Use this to your advantage, remembering that other candidates probably will not be practicing as diligently as you are, giving you the upper hand.

If you do not have access to a career center, practice interviewing with a friend and record yourself so you can critique it afterward for areas of improvement. Use the list of standard interview questions located at the end of the chapter on interviewing for the practice interviews.

You can also ask your professors if they know of any businesses that would be open for conducting a mock interview with you. They should be able to put you in touch with a few businesses they have worked with in the past. Have you ever thought of just asking a business if they would be willing to do a mock interview? If you asked me, I'd do it. That would set you apart from the crowd, and if you do a great job, they may even put you in touch with someone they know who might be interested in hiring you. Don't waste their time, and don't expect a written summary of your interview. At the end of the interview, ask them for feedback on areas that they think you should focus on, and take their advice.

IV. CAMPUS INTERVIEW DAY

Most campuses will have interview days where they invite various businesses to campus to interview students. This is convenient for the business because they can interview six to ten students in a single day, the career department will organize the event, and the business will get some promotion at the college.

Students can review the business's job listings in advance and then add their names to the interview list if they are interested. Typically, there are no requirements to fulfill before adding your name to the list, so this is a guaranteed way to get an interview with a business.

Use interview days as a way to practice interviewing. I suggest you review each business, and if there is any chance that you would consider working for them, add your name to the list. The worst that will happen is that they won't follow up with a second interview.

In the next chapter I am going to cover the interview itself, and all of that advice applies here as well. However, there are a few minor things that you can do during the campus interview day that will easily and quickly set you apart. Let's cover those here.

Interview Order is Important: Since the business will probably be interviewing up to a dozen student candidates, getting the first or second slot is critical to hold their attention. I've done this many times, and it is exhausting, so those last few candidates of the day do not get the same attention as the first.

Set Yourself Apart From Your Classmates: While at other job interviews you will be competing with similar candidates, at a college interview day, you will be competing with your classmates. You have all taken the same classes, worked on the same projects, and are largely indistinguishable on paper. Talk mostly about non-school projects to help set yourself apart, and take that advantage since you've built a portfolio of work already.

Expect the Interviewer to Know Your Professors and Curriculum: While this is not true for every business that interviews at a campus, I will also do my research in advance to know the curriculum and the professors. Assume that I can and will ask the professors about your participation and skills, so take the effort to let your professors know that you are interviewing with businesses, that way they may mention the additional work you have been doing or how you've impressed them on a project. As I mentioned earlier, networking is critical and businesses are networking as well.

Research the Companies: I go into this in greater detail in the next chapter, but trust me, most other college students aren't even going to look up the company that they are interviewing with, so you have a huge advantage just by doing a little research.

V. UNUSUAL STRATEGIES FOR LANDING AN INTERVIEW

Landing an interview with the companies you want to work for can be tough. Chances are a lot of other people want to work there too, and their list of interviewees will be long. However, this entire book is geared toward helping you prepare the experience, brand, portfolio, and skills necessary to be ready for the interview when it comes along. To actually land the interview, though, there are two unusual and unexpected strategies that can help you get your foot in the door.

Strategy One: This is a technique that is almost guaranteed to get you an interview or meeting, but it's also one virtually no one will do.

Step 1: Look up who runs the organization.

Step 2: Using a piece of nice stationary, handwrite a short note explaining your value proposition to the organization and why you think they should hire you.

Step 3: Mail the note along with your résumé to the person who runs the organization.

Step 4: Make sure you are prepared for the interview, because that will open the door for you to sell yourself.

I know it sounds too simple, but trust me: it will get their attention. You may not get offered a job for many reasons—perhaps they are not hiring or your skills are not in alignment with what they are hiring for, but it will give you the absolute best chance possible. They may even pass your résumé and a recommendation to another department or business for consideration.

Writing a value proposition may sound intimidating because it is not something taught in school. Put yourself in your future employer's position and ask yourself why they should hire you. What are the advantages of you over the other candidates? How do you bring value to the organization? What value do you bring to the table?

Here is a simple example (keep in mind that they have your résumé so don't just repeat your skills in the note):

Dear [Mr./Ms. Boss],

I have been researching your company and would love the opportunity to interview for the [position]. As you can see from my enclosed résumé, I am passionate about [career] and have built a compelling portfolio of work that you can view [here].

I bring [name value] along with a passion to continue to grow and learn.

I look forward to meeting you in person soon. My contact information is on my résumé.

Thank you,
[You]

Strategy Two: Have you ever considered taking your laptop and just showing up at a business that you want to work for and asking them if you can hang out for the day? Probably not, but what if you did?

To be fair, you should probably call first, because you'd hate to stop in on a day when they have a huge client meeting or right before a major deadline.

Let's say you call or e-mail in advance and say something like this:

Dear [Mr./Ms. Boss],

"I'm a recent college graduate and looking for the right business with a great company culture. I've been working on my portfolio and thought it would be helpful if I could stop by and see how your company works. Maybe I could hang around for a bit and see how your developers interact with each other, maybe even contribute an idea or two? I'd love to learn more about your business, I won't be a nuisance, and I have work to keep me busy while I observe. What do you think? Are you open the idea?"

Thank you,

[You]

They may say no, or they may never reply. But what if they said yes? What if you got to know all of the developers and the management? Are they even hiring? Probably not, but they might be in the future.

I ran this scenario by a few businesses, and they all agreed that they would probably invite someone to come in for the day in that situation. They'd set you up in a spare cubicle and welcome you to their business.

After you've spent the day with a business, follow up with a handwritten thank-you note and see what happens.

Now Go Execute

- Take advantage of your school's career center resources.
- Sign up for early internship interviews to help practice your soft skills.
- Ask for a mock interview.

8

THE INTERVIEW

Congratulations—you've done it! You have prepared your website, work portfolio, and social media profiles. You wrote a killer résumé, promoted yourself, built your authority, and networked like a pro. You polished your interview skills, tweaked your pitch, reviewed the company's background online, and landed an interview at your dream job. You are now ready for the interview.

To perform well at this all-important stage, you need to know what to expect during the interview. Most businesses will perform a phone interview first to eliminate as many candidates as possible because it is expensive to bring a candidate in for an interview. That's right: the phone interview is a technique to eliminate candidates. A phone call can easily be ended if the candidate is not doing well, so they can commit to ten minutes, but an in-person interview will typically last thirty to sixty minutes and is awkward to just end after ten minutes. It is critical that you get past the phone interview and land that in-person interview.

You have sent out your résumés and know that the dream career opportunity may be calling you at any minute, so be prepared to accept that call. Every call that you get could be that call. Chances are they will e-mail you first, but you never know, sometimes they just call out of the blue to see how you handle yourself. Answer every call professionally, not with a "yo" or "'sup," answer it like a professional would, say something like, "Hello, this is [name]."

I. THE PHONE INTERVIEW

Phone interviews can be very uncomfortable and tricky because you must rely entirely on audio for cues. You will not know if the interviewer is looking puzzled by one of your answers and you will lose any body language feedback.

Typically, you will first receive an e-mail from a prospective employer asking you for a time to set up a phone interview. Make sure you work on their schedule as much as possible; do not suggest that they call you at seven p.m. on Monday or on a Saturday afternoon because there is a good chance they will simply eliminate you from consideration. Make sure that you are able to set up a time for the interview when you can be in a private and quiet location to focus entirely on the phone interview. Do not take the call from your car or in a coffee shop if you can avoid it, since you won't be able to focus in those situations well.

Depending on the size of the company, the phone interview will either be done by someone in human resources or someone in the department that is actually hiring for the position. You need to figure this out as quickly as possible, because your call goals will be different depending on the position of the person you are talking to.

If you're being interviewed by human resources, you need to keep your answers short and accurate, and never answer anything that would eliminate you as a candidate. Questions will typically be about your experience only, like if you are familiar with a specific technology or program. Answer positively even if you are not familiar, but do not lie and say you are an expert when you are not. Instead, say that you are not familiar with that particular technology but it is something you are very eager to learn, or that it is similar to another technology that you are very proficient with. Human resources will simply be running you through a checklist, so make sure you check off all the boxes in a positive way. Your only goal at this point is to get a callback for an in-person interview.

Human resource members are usually not technical professionals, so make sure you don't accidentally confuse them with your answers. Try to keep each answer short and concise, something that is very easy for them to jot down on the job questionnaire form that they are reading from (yes, they are filling out a form on the other end of the phone). Whenever possible, provide a simple answer, then elaborate briefly, and finally restate the simple answer so they can write it down.

If the person doing the phone interview is from the actual department doing the hiring, you have a wonderful opportunity to dive deep into your portfolio and knowledge. Don't hold back on your experiences, and feel free to elaborate on every question asked. Questions will typically be more technical, so use this opportunity to drill into your work experiences. The questions usually are just off the cuff as well, not prepared in advance. If they ask about a technology or program that you are not familiar with, do not lie about it, but rather discuss similar technologies with which you are proficient and how your past experience will be very valuable.

Always be conscious of how long you are taking with each answer. Avoid rambling on or focusing too much on one topic. Everyone has a short attention span, so keep your answers concise and clear, and always ask if they have any follow-up questions if you think you are getting off topic. If you think you are rambling, you probably are, so wrap it up and restate the original answer; hopefully you remember what it was.

Your only goal of a phone interview is to land that in-person interview. People are rarely, if ever, hired based on a phone interview alone. Set the stage as to what they would expect from you during an in-person interview. Explain that you can show them your portfolio of work during an in-person interview. Hold back a bit on diving too deep on a phone interview, and allude to being able to show them instead of telling them about your work while in person.

It is perfectly fine at the end of the phone interview to ask if you can do an in-person interview. They will probably not commit, but it shows your interest in their organization and the job itself. Simply ask something like, "Thank you for the opportunity for this phone interview. Can I set up an in-person interview to go deeper into my portfolio?"

II. THE IN-PERSON INTERVIEW

You are now ready for the interview that could launch your career. You have made it this far, and now is your time to show that you're the perfect candidate for your dream job. Let's start with a list of things to do.

- **Be Honest and Genuine.** Be genuine about your skills and knowledge. The last thing you want to have happen during an interview is to make up a skill that inevitably will be revealed during the post-interview review as being false. That will eliminate you from consideration for sure.
- **Be Confident.** Confidence is one of the best assets you have. If you demonstrate confidence, it shows that you are someone who will bring value to the organization. No one wants to hire someone who lacks confidence in themselves or what they can accomplish.
- **Scout the Location the Day Before Your Interview.** Find out how long it will take you to get to the interview, and anticipate extra traffic that may occur as well. Know which building and room you'll be in if possible, and which person you are meeting. Do not try to figure this out the day of your interview. Also, make sure you can pronounce the person's name you are interviewing with. Write the information on a small piece of paper so you do not stress out about the interview and forget the person's name.
- **Review the Company's Website and History.** Know enough about the company that you can answer the question, "What do you know

about our company?" It will come up, so be prepared. Many other candidates won't have a solid reply, so this is an opportunity for you to set yourself apart from the others. Research the company and prepare a few sentences in advance so you come across as well-prepared.

- **Dress Appropriately.** Exactly what that means will vary based on the company, culture, region, and the type of job that you are applying to. If you are unable to determine the appropriate attire, error on the side of more formal. During your scouting, see what others are wearing and dress slightly nicer than that. It is perfectly fine to wear a suit or dress to any job interview; you will never lose points for overdressing. Dressing nicely will naturally give you confidence, and you need every bit of confidence to land this job. If you scout out the location the day before, note what people are wearing.

- **Bring Your Laptop.** You may not need it—in fact you may not even be able to get online—but it does show that you are taking the interview seriously and are more than willing to demonstrate your skills, knowledge, and portfolio if necessary. Be prepared to demonstrate your portfolio offline.

- **Bring Multiple Hardcopies of Your Résumé.** Bring at least three identical copies of your résumé. It is best to have a copy in front of you during the entire interview so you can quickly refer to it when asked a question. You may not remember exact dates of an employment, so it is better to simply look it up than to stumble over an answer.

- **Bring Your Portfolio in Hardcopy.** This is a bit tricky if you have thousands of lines of code, and you don't need to bring them all. But definitely bring a hardcopy to demonstrate your portfolio. Examples would be to print out some of your code, websites, or your profile page from GitHub. Plan on leaving everything behind for your future employer to review. Put everything in a folder with your name and phone number prominently displayed. Make it easy for them to contact you if they have questions.

- **Bring a Notebook and Pen.** At the start of the interview, confirm you have everyone's name and title correct and jot them down in your notebook. That way you can refer to them by name throughout the interview with confidence. Everyone loves to be addressed by their name, so occasionally use their first name during the interview. Write down every program or technology they ask you about. This will prepare you for a second callback interview if one happens.
- **Prepare a Two- to Three-Minute Overview of Yourself.** In addition to the ice-breaker overview, you should have a bullet list of topics you want to make sure gets covered during the interview. You may also want to jot down questions you have for them, because this demonstrates that you are very organized and prepared.
- **Make Absolutely Sure Your Phone Will Not Make a Peep During the Interview.** No beeping, buzzing, or chimes. Turn it completely off if necessary or leave it in your car. While it is not the end of the world if it does happen, it is embarrassing and will throw you off for the rest of the interview if it does ring.
- **Review Standard Interview Questions.** I prepared a list of standard interview questions in this chapter, so make sure you can answer each of those questions without hesitation.

At the start of the interview, quickly get comfortable and don't shuffle around papers or act unprepared. Put 100% of your attention on the interview. Try really hard to remember everyone's first name.

Typically, the interview will start with a few ice-breaker questions. They may speak a bit about who they are or their company's background; however, they may also just jump right in and see how you handle the pressure, so be prepared. Have at least a two- to three-minute overview about yourself prepared and then jump right in to the interview. Speak clearly and at an easy pace. If you find yourself speaking too fast or too loud, just adjust yourself and go on. If there are multiple people conducting the interview, try to look at them both and address them both throughout, even if one clearly has more seniority. Even if one of

them never says a word, treat them as if it is equally important to get their approval to hire you.

As the interview progresses, keep a checklist of all the items that you wanted to cover. This should include all of your portfolio work you have prepared, as well as the items outlined on your résumé. Mark each item off once it has been covered, so that way you won't repeat yourself over and over. Simply refer back to past items discussed.

Repeating the same story or work history multiple times will catch their ear as an echo. It is best to avoid repeating yourself, so have multiple experiences and projects to talk about.

Remember, the interview is about you, your skills, and how you would fit into the company's culture, so keep that the focus. You prepared for this, now is your time to shine.

Now Go Execute

- Line up a few interviews to get used to the process.
- Learn from every interview that you do, and note what resonates with those doing the interviews.
- Keep an eye out for feedback during each interview, since it will be there. Take advantage of that feedback and adjust your delivery, résumé, and flow.
- Always ask questions about what they look for in entry-level candidates, since chances are others are looking for the same skills.

III. STANDARD INTERVIEW QUESTIONS

You can never predict all the questions that you may be asked during an interview, but there are some that come up frequently, so you might as well be as prepared as possible. Study these questions, record your answers, and practice what you will say. If you can ace the easy

questions, you will have more confidence when you get hit with an unusual question. Even if you mess up on a few questions, having confidence overall will save you.

When answering questions, make sure you explain the "how," not just the "what." Pretend that your answers are explaining to the interviewers how to complete a task. If you're asked about a past accomplishment, explain how you solved the problem, not the basic fact that you eventually solved it.

Questions to Expect

1. *Describe yourself.* This is almost always the first question during an interview. Use the personal brand summary you wrote in the branding chapter. Make sure you do not stumble on the first question; practice how you will answer and nail it during the interview. Since it is likely the first question, this will set the tone for the rest of the interview. Remember to breathe and speak clearly with confidence.
2. *Where do you see yourself in [one, five, ten, fifteen] years?* This is obviously a loaded question, and if the tables were turned, they probably could not answer the same question. Prepare your answer, be insightful and genuine, and don't say something like, "I'm going to be doing your job." For the record, I never ask this question of candidates.
3. *What do you know about our company?* You better have something good here, since it shows that you took the effort to actually look them up online and read a bit. Don't go too deep, since they know what they do, but pick out a few tidbits and demonstrate you researched them and their senior management.
4. *What is your dream job?* You already have an answer for this because you wrote one out during the career planning section. Answer honestly but don't box yourself into a corner by describing the job of

the person who is interviewing you, since they may see it as a threat or pandering.

5. *What are your strengths and weaknesses?* Another great loaded question. Don't say that you have no weaknesses, since that sounds arrogant, and don't say your strengths are also your weaknesses. And definitely don't make yourself sound like you have a ton of weaknesses. Think of an answer in advance and be prepared to explain yourself well.

6. *Why did you apply for this job?* This sounds easy enough, but it is difficult to answer without sounding like you are applying for any possible job on the market. Pick a few things that you genuinely like about the company and position, stick with those. Don't make it sound like you are applying for just any job.

7. *Explain a project or accomplishment that you considered a success.* You now have a lot of projects to lean on since you've built your portfolio. It would be good to prepare an answer for this one since it gives you a great opportunity to explain in greater detail some of your accomplishments. Speak clearly, with as little jargon as possible.

8. *Explain a time when you made a mistake.* We've all been there, so pick one in advance and prepare your answers. Don't try to wing one on the day of the interview because you may go down a path that you should not during an interview. Be genuine with your answer.

9. *If I were to ask your former employer/professor about your weaknesses, what would they say?* This is a good one because you don't know if they know your past employer or professor. Think about what they would say, or better yet, ask them now, before you interview.

10. *What do you do in your free time?* Think before you speak, and don't offer up hobbies or activities which may come off as offensive to someone you are interviewing with. If one of your hobbies is gambling all weekend in Las Vegas, you should probably

describe a different past time. This gives you a chance to show that you're human, so don't say, "I only work" either. Be genuine in your answer.

11. *What questions have I not asked you?* There is a really good chance that you'll get this question. Depending on how thorough your interviewers have been, you very well may have covered everything that needed to be covered. If not, go ahead and explain past projects and your portfolio.

12. *What questions do you have for us?* Always have a few questions that you save for the end of the interview. The next section covers some great questions, but don't ask them all. Pick the ones that are the most important for you, and ask just those. Pick two or three questions.

Questions to Ask Interviewers

1. What exactly would my day-to-day responsibilities be and who will I report to?
2. What resources does the company provide to allow staff to learn, grow, and advance?
3. What did the last person that left the company give as his or her reason for leaving?
4. What are the company's greatest assets?
5. What can you tell me about your company's growth?
6. What skills and characteristics do you value most in someone for this position?
7. Could you describe a typical day for someone in this position?
8. How will this position be graded on success in the next six months?
9. What is the biggest challenge facing the organization today?
10. How would you describe the company's culture?

11. How would you describe your management style?
12. What do you like best about working for this organization?
13. How has this position evolved since it was originally created?
14. What are the qualities of successful managers in this organization?
15. Did you have any hesitations when reviewing my résumé?

IV. SENDING A FOLLOW-UP

This may be something you haven't heard of people doing, but it provides you an option to set yourself apart from others—after each interview, send them a follow-up thank-you note. It does not need to be complicated. It can be just an e-mail thanking them for the opportunity to be interviewed and leaving the door open for them to ask any follow-up questions. If anything was left unresolved during your interview, like a question that you could not answer, now would be a great time to fill in the gaps with a short answer. Include a digital copy of your résumé and a link to your online portfolio website, making it easy for them to pass this information to their colleagues.

I would suggest that you follow up with an actual handwritten thank-you card instead of an e-mail. A card should be simple with a few words thanking those who conducted the interview. Again, it will set you apart from all the other candidates that interviewed with them. Do not expect a card to fix a bad interview, but it will help a good interview.

Avoid asking them follow-up questions in your thank-you note, and make the communication one direction only—you are sending them information. This is meant to be a thank-you note, not a conversation. They probably won't answer any questions you ask, anyway. It is fine for them to follow up with you if they want, and in fact that is great, but don't load the e-mail or note with a question that you want answered. If you have an actual question, wait a few days and then send a separate e-mail asking for clarification.

Send the e-mail or card the same day as the interview to keep the communication open. Take the time to review grammar and spelling, since the last thing you want to do at this critical point in the interview process is to give them a reason to reject you from consideration.

Now Go Execute

- Always send a follow-up note by e-mail or card after each interview.
- Take this opportunity to answer any missed questions asked during the interview.
- Don't use a thank-you note as a way to ask questions, since they probably won't reply anyway.

V. SOCIAL MEDIA UPDATES DURING THE INTERVIEW PROCESS

During the interviewing process, you may be evaluating multiple job opportunities. It is always a good idea to have options, allowing you to pick the career you want instead of taking the only offer you receive. This can be tricky because you don't want to delay one opportunity before another opportunity is certain. The best way to handle this situation is to start interviewing before you graduate with companies that you are interested in pursuing. Since you probably have not graduated yet, you have an artificial buffer of a few months to make a decision. Waiting until you graduate will force you to accept or reject each offer as they come along, not knowing what the next option may look like.

Keep every job interview that you conduct confidential to avoid companies finding out that they may be pursuing the same candidate. Don't lie and say you are not interviewing anywhere else, because they may already know that you have interviewed with others. Instead, explain that you are hand selecting the companies that you are interviewing with to pick the career opportunity that best fits both parties. Being honest and genuine will go a long way in building trust.

While you are interviewing with prospective employers, keep complete radio silence on all of your social media channels, even filter the information that you may share with friends as they may talk about your interviews with others. It is best to keep all interviews completely confidential until all parties have negotiated and signed a letter of intent.

Do not post anything about your interviews or prospective job opportunities. Do not follow the companies that you are interviewing with on social media, either, as this may tip your hand. If you receive connection requests from someone that you interviewed with, simply hold off on accepting their invite until after you have accepted the position.

Even after you receive a job offer, it is advisable not to make any changes or comments about your future employer until after your first day of work. Far too often the process will break down between the initial job offer and the actual start date. You may think it is a done deal once the company makes an offer, but things can happen.

Now Go Execute

- Keep confidential all of your interviews and company discussions with everyone.
- Do not post on social media that you are interviewing with any specific company.
- Do not accept friend requests from companies that you are interviewing with until after you have accepted a job.

9

NEXT STEPS

You made it to the end, you just crushed your job interview, and now you are ready to receive that job offer or else the rejection notice. Either way, you are better prepared now than ever to start your career.

You might think that every business is well organized, ready to bring on new employees, and has all of their paperwork in order for you to join them on day one. But that's often not the case. A friend of mine, who was working for a very fast-growing company at the time, ran into an interesting conflict. After one of their employees left, they realized that they did not have the proper paperwork in place to ensure employees did not take trade secrets with them when they left. This meant that they had to retroactively get all of their engineers to sign off on ownership and confidentiality on all intellectual property that had been developed. That made from some awkward conversations.

In this chapter I will cover those next steps, what to do with the job offer, how to accept the offer, what documents to expect, and even what to do if you do not get an offer. And if you are sweating spending forty years in the same job, you shouldn't be. People are changing jobs and careers more than ever. It is said that millennials are expected to change industries multiple times during their careers. With your education with coding, your career options are endless.

I. RECEIVING A JOB OFFER

Congratulations, you just received a job offer! You made it. Well, almost. Let's review the process before we celebrate your success.

A job offer is just that: an offer. It is not the final answer and it is not the only option you have. If you have done everything that I have outlined so far, you might land multiple job offers, so let's not jump on the first offer you receive. Everything in life is negotiable, even your first job offer. I am not advocating that you negotiate just for negotiation's sake, but you need to make sure you are getting what you want. This is a big decision, possibly the biggest decision you have ever made. In fact, most of the time, the job offer will be fair and you should have no need to negotiate.

Keep in mind that a job is a trade of your most valuable asset—your time. You are trading your time for money. You have a finite amount of time each day, therefore you need to make sure you are being compensated accordingly for this asset. The best time to negotiate your time's value is before you sign the dotted line. It will be exponentially more difficult to negotiate after your first day.

This may be the first job offer you have ever received and you may not know what to expect. The documents may look very formal and final, maybe even intimidating. A good job offer will include, at minimum, the following terms, sometimes explained in confusing language:

- A job description along with who you will report to—i.e., your new boss.
- Your initial salary compensation, possibly with an introductory or probationary period defined. Usually there will be no confusion as to the compensation offer and will either be in an hourly or annual dollar amount. (There are roughly two thousand working hours per year, so do the math if you want to convert it one way or the other.)

- Some job offers will define a probationary period where you or the employer may decide to part ways without any explanation or obligation. Laws vary from state to state on what can and cannot be done during the probationary period. Don't be afraid or offended by a probationary period, because they are very common and used at all job levels. Plus, it is in your best interest to part ways early if the job is simply not working out.

- An outline of policies on paid time off, vacation, and sick leave. Sometimes this is not included, but you should make sure you understand them as part of your compensation. One week of paid vacation is about 2% of your annual salary.

- Health, dental, and retirement benefits package, and an explanation on when and how you would qualify for each. It is common to tie benefits to employees only after the first ninety days of employment. This may mean you need to plan ahead to avoid a gap in your own insurance coverage. If benefits are not discussed, make sure you ask before accepting any job offer.

- An employee agreement, nondisclosure agreement, noncompete agreement and/or nonsolicitation agreement. These will look very formal and may be intimidating, but don't worry, we will cover them next.

Because this is your first job, you may be nervous about how to proceed. The best path is to take your time, review all of the documents, take notes of items that you do not understand, and ask them to explain anything that is confusing before you sign. It is unlikely that you will need an attorney, so don't sweat the documents either.

The first thing you want to do is look at the parts of the offer that are the most valuable to you. Is that your salary, your paid time off, your ability to advance in your career, the company's culture, or the experiences you will gain over the years? If you are comparing multiple job offers at once, you may need to create a list of the pros and cons of each offer.

Think about the full package as its whole value, and do not focus on salary alone. One company that has a matching retirement plan could boost your overall compensation significantly over another without a matching plan. You must look at all of the numbers to get the full picture of your compensation and benefits. The following table will help calculate your true compensation:

Benefit	Add or Subtract Dollar Value
Annual salary	+ (value)
Health care paid by company	+ (value)
Health care paid by employee	− (value)
Annual PTO (calculate hourly)	+ (value)
Retirement plan	+ (value)
Transportation to work	− (value)
Education reimbursement	+ (value)
TOTAL	Sum

Typically, a job offer will have an expiration date associated with it so that you must make a decision within a few days to a week. If you are being rushed to make a decision, that might tell you something about the company's overall attitude toward its employees. A week is reasonable but if you know that you cannot commit within their time frame, you should have a really good reason to ask for an extension. Do not try and leverage one job offer against another—you will lose in the end, and trust me, that is no way to start your career. You would be surprised at how quickly information goes from one company to another, even if they are perceived competitors. Many executives belong to common networking organizations and will talk, so don't be the person who thought they could outwit two businesses.

Always be genuine with your intentions and you won't have issues negotiating.

Many employers will take offense if you counter with a higher salary, especially if you are right out of college with virtually no work experience. Often times, the people who make the offer, especially for entry-level positions, do not have the authority to adjust the offer being made, which means they now have to prove to their boss that you are worth more money. If you feel strongly that you are being undervalued, you may have done a poor job presenting yourself during the interview. Instead of asking for a larger salary, ask for a sixty-day compensation review as part of your job offer, allowing you to prove your value. Of course, you actually have to prove your value or you can expect a very poor outcome. Make sure you get the sixty-day review added to your employment agreement as well, because often they will "forget" that they agreed to that condition.

When entering college, you may have been told by advisers, counselors, and professors what to expect as an average starting salary upon graduation. Remember that they want you to complete your degree, and that is their end-goal, not for you to land the highest paying job possible. Real-world experience, your ability to sell yourself, and the current job market will dictate exactly what your true value is upon graduation. Sites like CareerBuilder offer "real-world" salary ranges, which are also extremely biased. Keep in mind that the market will swing dramatically from one month to the next depending on the demand for new employees. Your value is what you make of it.

It's not uncommon to see a ten- to twenty-thousand-dollar salary difference in the job market for entry-level engineers from year to year. The demand will stretch through the entire industry. If a demand for those with ten-plus years of experience exists, it will create a vacuum for entry-level engineers as well.

Another area worth pursuing during your negotiation is asking for additional paid time off. Paid time off may be presented as the company's policy such that everyone gets ten days their first year. If you value your off time, consider countering their offer with the same salary but with fifteen days of paid time off instead of ten. Those additional five days will equate to about a 2% pay raise. Remember, each day you are off is a day that your employer is paying you but not receiving anything in return. Make sure you don't abuse this relationship.

Watch out for complex employee stock options. If the company is well established and publicly traded, the stocks could be sold and made liquid if you choose to leave in the first few years. However, if it is a privately held company, you may end up just forfeiting all of your stocks entirely if you leave, or are fired. Stock options are great, but you must understand their value and that they may actually be worthless under virtually every outcome.

II. BENEFITS

Your job offer should include a section on the benefits included. Some benefits may not be available until after a probationary period, typically ninety days, while others may be available immediately. Health benefits usually are not available on your first day of employment, so make sure you remain covered under your previous plan until the new benefits are available.

Benefits vary significantly from one company to another and can sometimes be very hard to measure. Health benefits may be offered but not paid for by the employer, or only a portion is covered by the employer, which is becoming the standard. Since rates can vary significantly based on the company's policy, make sure you know what your deductibles and copay will be in addition to your monthly premium costs. If your costs are unreasonably high, ask if the employer has other health benefit options. Sometimes you can buy your own policy for less than the one offered through your employer. After all, insurance premiums are calculated based on age (the older you are, the more expensive the premiums), and since you are young, you may be surprised at how little insurance policies could actually cost you.

Paid time off, or PTO, will often lump vacation and sick time into a single block of hours and not make a distinction between the two. This will work in your favor if you are not prone to taking a lot of sick leave. Ask when the PTO hours start to accrue as well as when they expire. Ask if you can run a negative balance through the year, what the approval policy is to use PTO time, and how much can be rolled over from year to year.

Flex time can also be a valuable benefit worth asking about during your job offer, especially if you will have a long commute. You may be able to work from home or a satellite office a few days a week, which will save you time and money. If flex time is not offered but you want the flexibility, it is best to get it included in your job offer rather than after you start your new job. Ask that any changes to the company's policy be written into your job offer so that they do not disappear on your first day of work.

Even though this may be your first job and you have a mounting list of student loans, do not skimp on the retirement plans offered by your employer. All employee match programs are worth participating in since it is like guaranteeing a 100% return on your investment. Start saving as soon as you can, because compounded interest over fifty years is a wonderful thing. If your company offers stock or stock options, seek guidance from a financial planner before committing, as you may be contributing to a plan that will never pay out.

III. ACCEPTING A JOB OFFER

While you probably have a deadline for your job offer, never accept as soon as the offer is made. Always take the offer home, review the details, and think about it. If the employer requires an on-the-spot decision, I guarantee you don't want to work for them. At minimum, think about it overnight, talk it over with a close friend, family member, or mentor.

Once you have negotiated your job offer and considered all of your alternatives, you are ready to accept an offer. Once you accept it, you will be agreeing to an employee intent contract, which just states that you agree to work for them in exchange for the terms agreed upon.

Make sure you are done negotiating all potential offers before you actually accept one. You wouldn't want to accept an offer from one company only to have another company offer you a better deal next week. While the employee intent contract is a legal contract and you will be expected to show up on the agreed upon date, these contracts are often broken by either party before the start date with little or no consequence at all. However, avoid getting yourself in a situation where this would occur, as it will likely have negative consequences later in your career. I have seen candidates sign an employee intent contract only to call the day before their start date to say that they have taken another job. In other instances, I have seen employees be hired only to find out on their first day that the person who hired them did not actually have the authority to make the offer in the first place—and they didn't have a job.

Typically, you won't have any further documents to deal with until your first day of employment. Your first day of employment will have a long list of things for you to review and sign. A list of common documents is covered in the job documents section next.

Upon accepting one job offer, you need to reject all the other job offers. Keep in mind that you may need to revisit them again in the future, so make sure you end all negotiations on good terms. You never know what is going to happen.

If you are talking to multiple companies, you may get a counter-offer after accepting one offer. This is going to be awkward, since you agreed to work for one company and a second company sweetened their offer for you to join them instead. While every situation is different, you may be tempted to take the better agreement, and that may indeed be the better option. Keep in mind, you will likely be burning bridges.

Over the years, I've seen a lot of instances where someone leaves a company to take another job only to return a week, month, or year later. Yes, it is awkward for everyone. But it happens more often than you think and no one will ever forget it. Never leave on bad terms, since you may be back before you know it.

IV. JOB DOCUMENTS

You have done it! You just scored the job that puts you on track for your dream career—congratulations! You worked really hard to get here, so let's make sure we lock everything down so you get what you deserve and there aren't surprises on day one at your new job.

Depending on the size of the company, you will see a wide variety of documents and policies when you arrive for your first day. I'm going to cover the most common documents you will encounter and explain them for you. I will also point out what to watch out for to avoid a mistake that can cause you trouble years from now.

In general, companies are not out to lock you in for life or try to screw you out of what you deserve, however, it can happen as an artifact of excessive policy. Remember, everything is negotiable and it is your future, so only compromise on what you are comfortable compromising on.

For example, if the standard policy is only ten days of PTO but you really want to spend six weeks in Europe each year, ask if you can take a percentage pay cut to offset the additional PTO days. If you are the candidate they are looking to hire, this is a very reasonable request and they should have no reason not to grant it to you. Win-win!

Here are some common human resource documents that you may encounter.

Employee Offer Letter: An offer of the terms in which you agree to work for a company in exchange for compensation. This typically is not signed by the future employee, but rather is just a document outlining what they are offering if you accept the employee agreement.

Employment Letter of Intent: An agreement that typically states that you agree to work for the company based on the outlined compensation. Both parties will sign this agreement and it is a legally binding document. However, until you show up for the first day and sign all the other employee documents, it could be terminated by either party without much recourse. This does happen on both sides, so don't celebrate too early.

Employee Handbook or Policy Document: An agreement that outlines all of the employer's policies for each employee. This might be an informal-looking document or a very legal-looking document, depending on the company. These are the policies that all employees are expected to follow at all times. An employee handbook will often be considered a proprietary and confident document, meaning that you may not get to see a copy until after you start. You can always ask for an early copy if you have concerns. In general, you should not have any major issues, but feel free to ask about things that you think are unacceptable.

Non-Disclosure Agreement: An agreement that generally states that anything you learn while working for the company may be confidential and cannot be shared with anyone outside of the company. Non-disclosure agreements, also referred to as NDAs, are very common for technical positions since they need to maintain their trade secrets if you ever leave or are terminated. NDAs can be complicated legal documents, but in general you should not have any issues signing one. If you have concerns, an attorney could review the document for a relatively small fee.

Noncompete Agreement: An agreement that generally states that if you should leave, or be terminated, you cannot work for a competing or competitor company for some period of time. These agreements are very common in sales positions since personal relationships are critical. Engineers are often required to sign them so that they cannot work for a competing company and reengineer trade secrets. These agreements are very tricky and very difficult to enforce. In general, you should not have any issues signing one. If you have concerns here, an attorney could review the document also for a relatively small fee.

Nonsolicitation Agreement: An agreement that generally states that if you leave, or are terminated, you cannot solicit any employees, customers, or partners at your new job for a period of time, typically one to three years. A nonsolicitation agreement prevents you from starting your own company with the intent of hiring top talent or stealing customers. These agreements are common in most industries, and in general you should not have any issues signing one.

Declaration of External Work: An agreement that generally defines how existing intellectual property or external projects will be handled now that you are employed by a new employer. These agreements are necessary if you did freelance work or work-for-hire before accepting your new position. Your existing clients may be folded into your new employer's book of business or you may continue to service them outside of your regular work schedule. Another area where this agreement will be important is your ability to continue to contribute to open-source projects during your employment. While this is a bit complicated, it should be something that can be mutually agreed to by both parties without a lot of work.

Termination Agreement: An agreement that generally defines the terms when you eventually leave the company. This agreement is often outlined when you start your employment so that everyone knows the process and rights if you choose to leave. Until you actually leave, the agreement is not executed. These agreements are not very common, but if you happen to run across one, now you know what it is for.

At any point in time if you think that an agreement sounds wrong or something is confusing, do not sign it! Ask for a copy so you can review it at your own leisure or with an attorney. As long as your intentions are genuine, there is no reason that your new employer would not grant you an option for a reasonable review. After all, no one wants to start a new job thinking that one of the parties is out to screw them.

Make absolutely sure that you receive a copy of every signed document and policy for your own records. Do not rely on the company to keep your copy for review in the future. If you need to review your legal rights before resigning, you do not want to have to go to human resources and ask for a copy of your paperwork. Get a copy today and store it a safe place for future use—do not blow that step off either. Keep your own copies.

I have seen situations where people are asked to resign from their position but have not kept their own copies of their employee agreement. This leaves them in an awkward position of having to make decisions based on their recollection of a document that was written years earlier.

While most business are efficient enough to retain good records of human resource files, I have seen instances where documents are lost or misplaced. Having your own signed copy can clear up questions or issues efficiently in those circumstances. This is especially useful if your job offer had special considerations that were not part of the standard employee agreement.

V. HANDLING REJECTION

Let's be honest—you won't get a job offer from every interview you do, no matter how well prepared you are. There are a lot of reasons why they might not offer you job that do not have anything to do with your qualifications or interview: maybe you are overly experienced, maybe they are looking for a specific skill set, perhaps they are not actually ready to hire anyone, or you might not be the candidate they are looking for. This is perfectly fine.

I have interviewed the same candidate multiple times, years apart, before offering them a job. Timing is everything, which is why preparing in advance is so important.

I had one candidate who would apply for a job every time I had an opening. He was a good candidate and he was passionate, but his specific skill set was not what I needed and I never did offer him a job. But I did recommend him for a job at another business, which did hire him.

You would be surprised how often that happens. When businesses find good candidates, they do talk about them to other businesses. I have gotten a lot of people interviews and jobs for other companies after they have interviewed with me. That is why it is so important keep rejections positive.

One thing to note about rejections is that most businesses will simply never call you back to tell you that they are not going to offer you a job. I think this is unfair and rude to the candidate, so I always follow up with every candidate. Plus, it gives me an opportunity to hear how they handle the rejection.

If the business does e-mail or call you to inform you that they have chosen another candidate, or otherwise decided not to offer you a job, it is best to thank them for the opportunity, and leave the door open for future positions. Say something like, "Thank you, I appreciated the opportunity to learn more about your business and I would be interested in applying again in the future if a new position opens up." Keep it simple, and do not try to defend yourself or inquire about why they chose someone else.

VI. WORKING IN THE INDUSTRY AS A WOMAN

Men have been dominating development careers for decades. We are starting to see some progress in getting more women to enter the field of developers and provide them with equal opportunities and support, but we have a long way to go.

I have interviewed many women over the years and have hired a number of them as well. Probably higher than the average business, but still nowhere near half. If you are a woman entering a developer career, you will likely find yourself working with a bunch of men.

Code Bootcamp, which I helped launch in 2015, has had a lot of women graduate. Our first two classes were made up of almost 50% women. This is compared to just a fraction of those who graduated with a computer science degree in nearby universities.

If you are a woman, I wish I could tell you that it will be easy, but it won't be. I recommend that you seek out a female mentor. It might take a while to locate one, but it will be worth tracking one down. Check with your university and ask if they could put you in touch with previous female graduates in your area. There are also great networking groups like Women Who Code. Having a great mentor group will keep you motivated. I need more female developers, and many other places do too, so don't let the challenges discourage you.

Female developers need to be bold and speak up during meetings when they have ideas. I have seen them be intimidated by their male counterparts too often, even though their ideas are just as valid. Be confident, speak up, and demonstrate your knowledge.

Interviews may be more difficult for women, especially if you are interviewing with a group of men. Speak with authority and confidence about your skills, experience, and portfolio. Also be prepared for tough questions, and then crush the interview. If they don't treat you with respect, you don't want to work there anyway. Take this opportunity to learn about them so you can be selective with the businesses that you are willing to accept an offer from.

VII. MOVING FORWARD WITH YOUR CODING CAREER

All of your hard work preparing your brand, experience, portfolio, and website has paid off. But the hard work is not over. You now need to plan your next advancement, preferably internal, at your new company. A few things you can do to prepare to move upward:

Define your next career goals and create a plan to execute them.

Keep your blog and portfolio updated with new work so you can demonstrate growth to your existing employer or prospective new employers.

Continue networking, both at your workplace and outside of it, since connections you have in the field can increase your value to your company as well as build your own personal network.

Always keep a portfolio of work you do outside of your day job; that NDA (nondisclosure agreement) you signed limits your ability to demonstrate to prospective employers the work you've completed during your work hours.

Finally, and arguably most importantly ...
Never stop learning!

MASTER CHECKLIST FOR SUCCESS

Below is a master list of items to work on as you start to clean up, create, and then build your brand and portfolio. If you are closer to graduation than a year or have already graduated, don't worry. It's never too late to start. Just work through these lists as quickly as you can, and consider pausing sending out résumés until you've worked through this list and the contents of this book.

ONE YEAR BEFORE GRADUATING

Social media platforms:

- Clean up Twitter or create account
- Clean up Facebook, set security preferences to "private"
- Create a LinkedIn account, and start to build your social network
- Identify social networking events in your community

Website:

- Create a personal website
- Create a blog associated with your career goals

- Feature portfolio work on your website
- Setup a GitHub account, check in your website resources
- Identify the projects that you want added to your portfolio
- Set up relationships necessary to build your portfolio
- Find related open-source projects that you want to contribute to, create accounts
- Draft your résumé
- Draft a résumé that you *want* to be able to submit to your dream job upon graduation

SIX MONTHS BEFORE GRADUATING

Social media platforms:

- Review your profiles to ensure nothing got posted that should not have been posted
- Continue to post business and career-related resources to all platforms
- Update your LinkedIn profile with your volunteer work and projects
- Build out your LinkedIn network with businesses to which you want to apply for a job
- Attend local networking events, be helpful wherever you can

Website:

- Increase blogging to weekly, make sure you have a backlog of posts ready to release
- Update your website to include your volunteer work and projects
- Link your GitHub and social networks to your website and cross promote

Portfolio work:

- Continue to post code and projects into GitHub; this needs to be your primary hub for code
- Contribute to volunteer projects
- Ask for references from your volunteer and portfolio projects
- Step up your open-source project work

Résumé:

- Update your résumé with the volunteer work and portfolio projects
- Update your education sections to reflect your anticipated graduation
- Update your desired job description and skill set upon graduation

ONE MONTH BEFORE GRADUATION

Social media platforms:

- Start to promote more about yourself, your projects, and your portfolio
- Keep everything career related, suspend personal posts for now
- Friend or follow key companies of interest and start watching what they are doing
- Attend as many networking events as possible, always be helpful and accommodating

Website:

- Advertise your skills through blog posts
- Update your website to reflect all of your volunteer work and projects
- Pick up your blog postings to be more career-centric

Portfolio work:

- Continue to post and promote your portfolio
- Polish any projects or code that you have been creating
- Review all of your code and projects, ask for references
- Promote your career goals with those within your volunteer and project work

Résumé:

- Write your formal résumé for use upon graduation
- Remove anything that is no longer applicable or accurate
- Proofread it!

UPON GRADUATION

- Celebrate! You deserve it!

AFTER GRADUATION

Social media:

- Continue to promote your work, skills, and career desires
- Ask for introductions to companies where you would like to work
- Connect with key individuals who may help you land a career
- Keep everything business, career, and industry centric
- Attend every networking event possible and promote your skills, desires, and projects

Website:

- Continue to promote yourself and your work
- Continue to blog and promote your projects

Portfolio work:

- Expand your portfolio as much as your time allows
- Add more volunteer or project work as necessary
- Focus on contributing to strategic projects based on the companies you wish to interview with
- Research companies where you would like to interview

Résumé:

- Continue to tweak and improve based on feedback

THANK YOU!

Thanks for joining me on this journey through your first career. I hope you found it useful.

If you loved the book and have a moment to spare, I would really appreciate a short review on Amazon. Also, please consider sharing this book with someone you know who is starting their career as a developer.

You can also receive a free worksheet guide here:
http://wiredforcoding.com/worksheet

ABOUT THE AUTHOR

William Bushee is an author, speaker, entrepreneur, educator, and overall technology lover. He cofounded Code Bootcamp of South Dakota where they teach web development to adults and video game development to kids.

You can connect with William on Twitter at @wbushee and e-mail him at william@wiredforcoding.com if you have questions or would like to book him to speak at your event, high school, or college.

For your free *Wired For Coding* worksheet guide,
visit http://wiredforcoding.com/worksheet